'There's Always Tomorrow'

Anna Neagle

Says

'There's Always Tomorrow'

AN AUTOBIOGRAPHY

W. H. Allen · London

A division of Howard & Wyndham Ltd 1974

FIRST PUBLISHED DECEMBER 1974
REPRINTED BEFORE PUBLICATION

© EVEREST PICTURES LTD, 1974

THIS BOOK OR PARTS THEREOF MAY NOT BE REPRODUCED
IN ANY FORM WHATSOEVER WITHOUT PERMISSION IN WRITING.

PRINTED IN GREAT BRITAIN BY
THE ANCHOR PRESS LTD, TIPTREE, ESSEX
FOR THE PUBLISHERS
W.H. ALLEN & CO. LTD
44 HILL STREET,
LONDON WXI 8LB

BOUND IN TIPTREE BY WM. BRENDON & SON LTD.

ISBN 0 491 01941 9

To Herbert
with love

Preface

Since the films about which I am writing will have been seen by many of the readers of this book, I have endeavoured to confine myself to happenings behind the productions. In the case of *Odette* the drama behind the scenes was almost overwhelming.

During my career I have been singularly fortunate in so many directions. Herbert gathered around him some remarkable talent, but since, for lack of space, it has not been possible to mention specifically many of those who have contributed so much to my success, both here, in Hollywood, Australia and New Zealand, I want to take this opportunity of expressing my appreciation and my thanks.

Extracts from the song *There's Always Tomorrow* are hereby reproduced by kind permission of Chappell & Co. Ltd.

A.N.

Chapter One

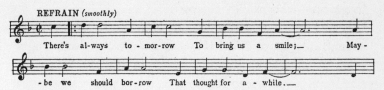

REFRAIN (smoothly)

There's al-ways to-mor-row To bring us a smile;— May-be we should bor-row That thought for a while.—

I NEVER hear that music, or recall those words without seeing the face of dear Jack Buchanan, sitting centre-back of the old London Hippodrome stage, perfectly relaxed, smoking a cigarette, humming a little and smiling at me encouragingly; urging me to forget the nervousness which so nearly ended my stage career before it was properly started.

The song is an 'oldie' of course, but not long ago a new L.P. was issued of Jack's best numbers and whenever I feel nostalgic I play it, and find my feet automatically weaving the old pattern, my head turning over my shoulder for one more glance at that encouraging smile.

Looking back it seems that almost everything good that has happened to me afterwards hung on the understanding and sympathy that lay behind it. I had made a complete mess of my audition, and I had no excuse. I was no inexperienced 'shooting star'. I had five years of hard chorus discipline behind me; first in André Charlot's Revues, later as one of C. B. Cochran's celebrated and much fêted 'Young Ladies'. I had even been to America, preceded by a flood of publicity. With one other girl I'd been singled out as 'the perfect English girl'. Cochran challenged the legendary Florenz Ziegfeld to produce a girl of his own to match us. Ruefully Ziegfeld admitted: 'English girls have a kind of refinement and poise that is lacking in most American girls.'

Whether 'refinement' is a desirable quality in a chorus girl I don't know. It seems an odd word to choose. What I found the American girls did possess was an ambition and drive to succeed such as I hadn't encountered before and, backing it up, a capacity for hard work that made our own tough time-table pale by comparison.

It was during that first visit to New York (appropriately enough in a show called *Wake up and Dream*) that I caught some of their determination to get to the top. When the time came to return to England, and Cochran offered me a place in the chorus of his next show, *Evergreen*, I turned it down.

'I've had five years in the chorus now,' I said. 'If I don't get out soon I never will.'

'Cocky' smiled at me. 'Well, I'm afraid, Marjorie, I haven't a part for you in *Evergreen*. If you want to stay in the chorus I'd be delighted – you're one of my best girls. But that's all I can offer you.'

He looked at me again, thoughtfully. 'Do you think you're really cut out for a stage career? Why don't you give it all up? Get married. Have a family. I feel that's what would really make you happy.'

Dear Cocky. How wrong could he be?

To give up at this point was unthinkable.

Nevertheless, when I left his office and the lift doors closed on me my knees were trembling. C.B.'s last words gave me a little comfort, but not much: 'If you ever want to come back into the chorus there will always be a place for you.' I must be mad to turn my back on such an offer. I wanted to stop the lift and run back. What held me back? A fear of looking too stupid? Or was fate taking a hand?

I saved a little money in America, about £70. A few days later I had regained some of my determination.

At least I'd have a go. I tried a little half-heartedly even before we left the States, but was quickly put off by mutters about Casting Couches.

Back in England I began to haunt the agents; a dismal, ego-destroying business if ever there was one. I was even auditioned by one of the famous Tait brothers who ran the entire theatre world in Australia and New Zealand. He was hardly encouraging. In 1972 I starred in *Charlie Girl* which broke all records at Her Majesty's Theatre, Melbourne – a Tait theatre!

Back in 1930 I did other auditions, all equally fruitless. One, I remember, was for Jack Hulbert.

I trailed out to the Elstree film studios too, and managed to get a few jobs as an extra. In *The School for Scandal*, starring Madeleine Carroll, I reached the dizzy heights of carrying a basket of flowers to her in one scene. But it was all very disheartening, and a little worrying. My money wouldn't last for ever and I didn't want to ask for help from my father, or brothers. After all, I had chosen to leave a well-paid job for this particularly hazardous life. And there were other reasons for my passionate independence at that particular time.

It was particularly galling to meet with so many rebuffs after five very successful years as a dancer in some of London's top revues and musicals. I had, frankly, been spoiled. When the 'Young Ladies' were first launched in the beautiful Coward revue *This Year of Grace, our* photographs appeared on the theatre bills, and *our* names, not just those of the stars. Heady stuff!

But I set my teeth. I was *not* going back to the chorus, I told myself grimly one night as I closed the door of another agent's office on the usual 'Sorry, dear, nothing today.' I glanced at the staircase up to the next floor. There was another agent up there. Was it worth a try? I glanced at my watch. Almost six o'clock. I turned away. Then I turned back and ran up the stairs.

Jean Clarbour looked up as I burst breathlessly into her office. 'I'm sorry, dear,' she began automatically. 'We're just closing, and anyway we're all fixed up for tomorrow.'

Then she looked at me again, her eyes narrowing slightly. 'Just a minute, though.' She disappeared through an inner door. I heard the mutter of voices. A moment later a man came out and looked at me too. I looked back, mystified and self-conscious.

Percy Clarbour gave his wife what seemed to be a meaningful little nod. 'Well, I haven't anything at the moment I'm afraid,' he said to me. 'But I'll see what can be done.'

My heart sank even lower as I walked down the stairs. I had heard that so often; and just for the moment it seemed . . .

What I did not know at the time was that Jean Clarbour had gone to tell her husband that something about me reminded her of a very successful silent film actress for whom they had found a great deal of work. It was little enough to go on, not much more than a hunch, but they decided to take a chance.

A few days later I was taken to see Sam Smith, of the original British Lion Film Company, who had a small part vacant in a film called *Should a Doctor Tell*, starring Maurice Evans who later went to America and became *the* great Shakespearean actor out there; and Norah Baring, who had made a big name in silent films.

I was given a film test, and got the part. Norah Baring was very kind. We had to provide all our own clothes in those days and I hadn't anything suitable for one scene, so she lent me one of her own dresses.

Once I'd broken through the icy surface, other things began to happen. My publicity photographs were noticed. I was asked to pose for advertisements, mainly for hats, stockings – things like that. 'Modelling' they call it today, and very highly paid, too. In those days it was a side-line for actresses and chorus girls making a little extra on the side.

Before I finished *Should a Doctor Tell* casting began for *The Chinese Bungalow*, with Matheson Lang as the star. Mr Clarbour sent for me again. 'Jill Esmond's playing the lead, but they're looking for a blonde to play her sister. It's actually a very good part. If you get it you'll be playing scenes with both Jill and Matheson Lang, but they don't want to pay for a "name" because with Matheson Lang they don't need anyone else to sell the picture. Their office is closed now, but I'm going to put your photograph under the door tonight. We'll see what happens.'

What happened, so far as I was concerned, was precisely nothing. No screen test, as I'd hoped. Then I found that, instead of doing a formal test, Producer-Director J. B. Williams and his Production Manager had been shown an actual scene from *Should a Doctor Tell,* so I had simply skipped all the nervous tension of a film test. They had talked to Maurice Evans, too, and he had kindly reported that I was 'promising'.

I'll always remember the day I signed that particular contract, partly because I felt it was such a step forward, and partly because there was a different kind of happiness and excitement in the air. I went to the office. There was Jill Esmond, who just had time to sign her contract before she and Laurence Olivier left on their honeymoon. They'd been married that morning. He used occasionally to call at the studios later to pick her up. My goodness, what a marvellous looking young man he was, and how bursting with personality. Anyone could see that he was destined for the heights.

After Jill left, Mr Williams and his Production Manager took me for what I naïvely thought was a celebratory cup of coffee at an ABC café not far from the office. When we were settled Mr Williams turned to me gravely. 'You know, don't you, that you are going to play with one of *the* great actors of the English theatre?' I nodded, dumbly. 'Well . . .' Mr Williams hesitated, as if seeking a way not to hurt my feelings. Then he went on: 'I think your name "Marjorie Robertson" has been too much publicised as a "Cochran Young Lady". Now you are turning to serious acting, you must change it.'

I stared at him. In my childhood, when I had day-dreamed of a stage career, I'd invented the most incredible professional names; but now I'd spent five years putting my real name on to playbills and programmes and didn't much like the idea of wasting all that publicity. I wasn't *ashamed*; I was *proud* of my success in the chorus.

'It's rather a long name, too,' Mr Williams went tentatively. His eyes twinkled. 'Think how many electric light-bulbs it would need outside a theatre!'

I was delighted at the very idea that it would ever come to that. But of course I was completely disarmed and I began to see his point. It was my own argument to Cochran in a way. If I'd remained 'Marjorie Robertson, Chorus Girl' much longer I would have been type-cast for life. This was just what I was trying to escape.

'My mother's name was Neagle . . .?'

'Nagle?'

'No – Neagle,' I protested.

'Don't worry – they'll call it Nagle,' he said.

'What about Anna Neagle?' I suggested.

'Oh, fine. That's just fine. Anna Neagle? That's it.'

And so Marjorie Robertson, successful chorus girl, was quietly, and a little sadly, disposed of in a tea-shop on the corner of Wardour and Old Compton Streets, on August 21st, 1930. And Anna Neagle, embryo actress and star, was born.

Chapter Two

I WAS Anna Neagle from the very beginning of my film career because *Should a Doctor Tell* and *The Chinese Bungalow* were released almost simultaneously.

Christopher Mann, the Public Relations Officer for *The Chinese Bungalow*, who later became a very big agent, had the same sort of hunch as the Clarbours. People were always telling me in those days that I 'had something', though they became vague about just what it was. I knew I was pretty and that I could dance well, but what this 'something' was no one seemed able to define. I have always felt myself that when I am in costume, made-up and on stage, I become a sort of changeling, quite different from my everyday self. But these people did not necessarily see me on stage. However, luckily for me, Christopher Mann decided to have me photographed by the great society photographers Dorothy Wilding and Janet Jevons, and they did a wonderful job. One of the photographs which appeared in the magazine *Spotlight*, the stage showcase for actors and actresses, was to catch the eye of someone very important in my life, almost at once.

It was Percy Clarbour again who called me to say there was a possible 'something in the air' for me if I'd like to come down to his office. I went – Jack Buchanan's Stage Director, Frank Smythe, was there. Mr Clarbour explained that Jack Buchanan was looking for a juvenile lead for his new show, *Stand up and Sing*. 'He won't want *me*,' I protested. 'I was in *Wake up and Dream* with him, in the chorus. He wouldn't even look at me.'

'We'll try one of those photographs on him,' said Mr Smythe. 'Anyway,' he added with a mischievous grin, 'you've changed your name, haven't you? I won't mention *Wake up and Dream* then you'll get off to a brand new start.'

But of course Jack was not as simple as all that. Apparently he remembered my doing one little thing on my own in *Wake up and Dream* – just carrying on a title-board before a sketch – but it was enough.

'Aha – so it *is* you! I thought I recognised the face, but couldn't place the name. Well, let's see what you can do.'

We went across to the Tiller school; a big, bare room where the famous Tiller Girls trained. It was cold, and I was frightened, terribly aware that although the films had helped a lot, this was my BIG chance and if I failed my career could be set back for years.

I was, like numerous other girls, madly in love with Jack, which didn't help. That wasn't as dramatic as it sounds. Every girl who ever worked within fifty feet of Jack Buchanan was madly in love with him. So were the Gallery Girls who waited patiently in queues, often for hours, outside the theatres to see his shows. So were the ladies who clattered their tea-cups through his matinees; and so was every other woman who had ever seen him on stage or film, or had heard his voice on records.

I'd taken extra singing and dancing lessons in New York, and worked *very* hard, especially at the new 'tap' routines which were only then beginning to creep into England. I had lots to show. I chose first a song I knew well, and a fairly simple dance; but my feet, which had kicked and tapped and pirouetted so blithely on half a dozen London and New York stages, were curiously leaden. And when I opened my mouth to sing nothing – but *nothing* came out.

I looked miserably at Jack.

'Come on, we'd better start all over again, hadn't we?'

'We' started all over again. 'We' tried everything we'd ever done successfully, and the result was awful.

Jack said nothing more than 'Put on your coat and hat. We'll go back to the office.'

I couldn't see much point in going back to the office to be told I was no good.

He picked up the little case with my dancing shoes in it and I tottered off beside him, back to his office at the Prince of Wales Theatre.

He sat down behind his desk. I collapsed into a chair.

'Well,' he said in a brisk, businesslike, voice, 'you're quite the best I've seen for this part, but you are so nervous I don't know whether you could possibly handle it.'

I pressed my sticky palms together in my lap.

'I must look for someone with more experience,' Jack went on patiently. 'If I don't find anybody within the next few days I'll give you a chance. I'll give you a definite decision at the end of this week.'

I'm sure Jack could never have known how I felt when he said that. It was rather like someone saying 'Pardon me if I turn the screw a little tighter each day . . .' And as each day passed, that endless week, my spirits sank lower. It didn't occur to me that if Jack had found someone else he would have let me know right away.

At the end of the week there was a telephone call from his secretary. 'Mr Buchanan wants to see you.'

Jack was smiling when I arrived. 'We're here to sign a contract,' he said.

I couldn't believe it. He must be mad!

He wasn't, quite. 'I'm taking you on tour, but it's entirely up to you whether or not you come into London.'

In the event it was not 'entirely up to me'. No one could have had more help, more patience, more understanding, more kindness. I must often have driven him to the very brink of exasperation by my lack of 'attack' on what was a very simple rôle. Everything was there to bolster my ego. I had beautiful dresses; I was playing with one of the most popular stage-idols of his day. The 'girls' could not have been sweeter, or more supporting. I was never for one moment aware of any jealousy or criticism from one of them, though many had danced with me before, in the chorus, and possibly some felt that, given the chance I was given, she could do very much better. The leading artistes were also very kind. Vera Pearce was a tower of strength – in every sense, and Morris Harvey and Richard Dolman were most encouraging. Two of the 'girls', the Farnham Sisters, were then as now my very dear friends.

We opened at the Southampton Empire, which was *enormous*. There were no microphones, no sort of amplification in those days. I often wonder what poor Jack must have thought after the Dress Rehearsal.

He sent for me when it was over, and I could see, even through the ghastly haze in which I was living, that he was dreadfully concerned about whether I would survive the Opening Night at all. And so we had a talk. A kindly talk, as always, on Jack's part; a teeth-chattering one on mine. And I did get through the Opening Night, thanks to his extraordinary generosity and ingenuity.

I had the big number with him, the theme song: *There's Always Tomorrow*. He had realised by now that the range was far too big for me. So he did the verse alone and we did just the chorus together. Then he moved, gracefully and unobtrusively, to the back of the stage and just sat on that bench, smoking, whistling a bit, swinging one leg and smiling at me; leaving me a whole refrain, and the whole of that big stage, to dance on my own. By now this was something I could do. He had arranged the routine to show me, and Eileen Adair's beautiful dress, to the very best advantage. By the time he rejoined me for the rest of the routine I was 'away'.

That should have been the end of my troubles. I should have gone on from strength to strength and triumph to triumph – if it hadn't been that waiting in the wings, or rather the hotel across the road from the theatre, was a mischievous imp in the form of a very well-known London agent.

We all went across to the hotel after the show for a meal. I went into the dining-room with Dorothy Robinson, a life-long friend from my Cochran days, and Sylvia Leslie, my step-mother in the show. The well-known agent was sitting just inside the door. He leaned forward as I entered.

'You did very well, dear.' The tone was patronising. 'But of course you're not coming to London, are you?' I stopped in my tracks, stunned. He went on chattily: 'Jack really wanted June for the part, but it wasn't big enough for her. I expect he'll build it up for her when he comes to London.'

I don't know to this day what lay behind his malice. Perhaps June was one of his clients. She was certainly a very big star at the time and had played often with Jack before, so the story was plausible. But it didn't need to be plausible to prick the fragile bubble of my newly-born confidence.

The tour lasted three months. We had three weeks at the Manchester Palace, then six weeks in Glasgow. I knew only too well that my main problem was one of 'projection'. Half in hope, half in despair, I decided to take extra singing lessons.

Despite the extra lessons, despite the assurances from colleagues, despite the obvious enjoyment and response of the audiences and the general success of the show, I went on worrying, and it showed. I became more and more miserable, and more and more nervous.

In the end Jack tackled Dorothy Robinson. What *was* the

matter with me? Dorothy told him about the rumours that I wasn't to go into London with the show.

'Who says she isn't going into London?' Jack snapped. And to me: 'Just stop listening to rumours. *I'm* the one who decides whether or not you go to London. And *I* think you will. In fact I've made up my mind that you will. I'll prune your part a bit more so that you can handle it without strain. And I'm having new dresses made for you. But,' he added warningly, 'it'll still be up to you. If you don't pull yourself together not only will you not open in London, you won't open anywhere else!'

It must have been a very worriyng time for Jack. It was possible he'd made the most appalling misjudgement in giving me the job at all. I realised that later; at the time I was too wrapped up in my own misery and nerves to think of anything, or anyone, else.

He brought his Front-of-the-House Manager, Frank Boor (a very celebrated and experienced man of the theatre indeed), as far as Newcastle to see me, and he endorsed Jack's judgement. I had, for them too, this mysterious 'something' everyone talked about, but no-one could define.

Elsie Randolph, the other Big Name in the show who had been starring in *Wonder Bar*, joined us at Birmingham, the last stop before London, and she added her praise and encouragement. Very slowly my shattered morale was repaired.

I don't, sadly, remember much about the Opening Night at the London Hippodrome, though I do remember being driven down from Birmingham by a friend on the Sunday night beforehand. He drove me straight round to the theatre and there my name was up – *In lights*! I remembered what J. B. Williams had said about my real name, and the number of light-bulbs it would consume. That was less than a year before.

Stand up and Sing was a typical musical comedy of its period:

frothy and frivolous. The music was charming but the 'book' unremarkable; the highly-involved plot frankly absurd. It was never meant to be anything but a bit of fun. Its success depended entirely on the playing, especially the timing.

Jack's sense of humour and timing could have made the proverbial telephone directory amusing, and he, with Elsie Randolph as his foil, carried it superbly.

Gordon Beckles on the front page of the *Daily Express* proclaimed: 'Theatrical London is talking about the young Cochran chorus girl whom Jack Buchanan selected as his new leading lady for *Stand up and Sing*. He took her from the chorus, encouraged her, dressed her and she made an instant success.'

One of the nicest things that happened after the first night of *Stand up and Sing* was a generous congratulatory telegram from C. B. Cochran, who had had such doubts about my ability to carry a part!

Cutting though the critics had been about the slightness and foolishness of the plot itself, it soon became clear that the audience did not agree with them. When Jack and I, as the two lovers, were to be finally parted I had to say 'What will you do now, Rocky?'

Jack's reply: 'I think I'll go to India and shoot Bombay Duck.'

Obviously a laugh line. We were more than a little disconcerted when for several performances no laughter came. Only after a while did Jack realise to his astonishment that it was *not* the audiences missing the humour. They actually *cared* about Rocky and Mary. From that night until the end of the long run, Jack cleverly played the scene in such a way that the whole improbable soufflé was important to them.

Jack took me to lunch at the Savoy soon after the London opening. I remember Hannen Swaffer, the Fleet Street columnist, coming across and saying in his blunt fashion:

'You're in the right hands with this man.' He never spoke a truer word.

Jack talked to me like a cross between a firm employer and a kindly uncle. 'You should be on the top of the world. You heard the audience at your curtain call. You've read the notices. You've given three performances in London and know that the Gallery Girls have taken you to their hearts. No need to remind you how important *that* is! So no more nonsense ... Hmmmm?' He raised a quizzical eyebrow and smiled. My heart turned a somersault as I shook my head obediently.

Despite my highly nervous state in the early days of *Stand up and Sing*, I did not miss one of the six hundred and four performances. So Roma Beaumont, who understudied me, never had a break. But it was not long before she was hailed as an 'overnight' sensation for her enchanting performance with Ivor Novello in *The Dancing Years* – and Richard (Dicky) Murdoch, getting his start in the show, was to become a household name. So great was Jack's flair that he had even engaged Anton Dolin for a spectacular classical dance in the midst of this frothy musical! And Charles Lefeaux, fresh from drama school, also appeared, though he was later to abandon the stage for a successful career as a producer.

Chapter Three

I CANNOT be the only four-year-old to have been scared by the snapping jaws of the crocodile in the stage version of *Peter Pan*, but possibly I was the only one to be carried out sobbing 'Don't let him eat my Daddy!' If you remember, Hook explains to Smee that the croc 'only ate Captains'.

My father *was* a sea-captain, and I adored him. When I saw him, that is. Most of my young life he was away, and for all I knew his long voyages took him to a Never-Never Land where hungry crocs lay in wait for unwary Captains.

Incidentally, I never saw the end of *Peter Pan* on stage until I played the title-rôle myself, many years later.

Autobiographies which dwell at length on childhood memories and family ramifications can, I know, be very tedious, but my ancestry, my immediate family and my early background were to influence my whole life, and later my work so much, and in so many different ways, that I must ask you to bear with me if from time to time I go back to things which I know meant a lot at the time.

I was the youngest of three, the only girl. Alan was almost nine years my senior, Stuart, three-and-a-half. So they really were Big Brothers. And I was a born hero-worshipper. There was my father, handsome, strong and wise, romantic in his uniform and so often away on Important Business in distant places; Alan, so much my senior he always seemed grown-up – equally handsome, good at games, light-hearted and gay; and Stuart, nearest to me in age, and later to share my artistic interests. Perhaps here, in hindsight, lies the biggest clue to my stage-fright. From my earliest recollection Stuart had one of the most glorious singing voices I've ever heard. One does not need to be a highly-trained psychologist to make a shrewd guess as to why, when the time came, I had difficulty in singing at all!

Stuart would have been appalled had he realised the effect his voice had on me. Luckily he never did. I loved to listen to him, and still do, on records. He died, tragically young, in 1958, but he left so much of himself behind, in music, in memory, in Sally his widow and my close friend, in his children Michael and Elizabeth, and *their* children; a continuing and growing delight.

Being the only daughter, as well as the youngest member of the family, I was no doubt dreadfully indulged. I was certainly always 'Daddy's Little Girl'. My mother was never physically strong. One of my earliest recollections is of her being pushed along the Promenade at Thorpe Bay in a bath-chair after one of her many illnesses.

Having brothers naturally I took to games. My favourite present from father was a cricket bat. Later I captained my school House at games. I saw the first West Indies Test Match in London, too, and the Australian girls playing the English – wonderful classical cricket. I even spent the day after my wedding at Lord's!

Although providing me with so much pleasure, I think my most embarrassing moment is tied up with cricket. During the filming of *Odette* in which Trevor Howard, who played Peter Churchill, turned out to be as keen a cricket enthusiast as Herbert and me, we made a date for the three of us to see the next Test Match – at the Oval. As was our custom we took a picnic lunch and sat in the sun instead of doing it in style in the Members' Stand. After lunch I thought I'd go and tidy up. The Oval is a great rendezvous – for men! Ladies having only recently begun to follow cricket in large numbers, the amenities are very limited. I searched near the Jack Hobbs Gate but there was only one 'Ladies' and a very long queue waiting. Since it was the only one I took my place at the end of the queue, prepared for a long wait. A middle-aged woman just ahead of me turned round, her eyes opened wide, 'Aren't you Anna Neagle?' she asked. I told her I was. 'You ought not to be here,' she said. 'Come to the head of the queue.' Before I could protest she literally dragged me by the arm to the top spot. 'This is Anna Neagle,' she told the ladies there, 'right at the end of the queue. You don't mind, do you?' she asked, as she put me at the head. There were murmurs of agreement and quite a flurry of excitement. All I wanted now was to get away. I had never been so embarrassed. But before I could excuse myself my turn came.

Word must have gone round, for through the open windows I heard a young boy shouting at the top of his voice, 'Come on, quick, Anna Neagle is in there – in the "Ladies".'

When I got out a mob of youngsters with autograph books were waiting and some of the obliging ladies also got out scraps of paper for me to sign. The party grew – although play had been resumed. I could not get away. Herbert left Trevor to look for me. He found me surrounded. 'They've lost another wicket,' said Herbert. 'I couldn't imagine what had happened to you.' I told him.

'That's one for your book,' he laughed, 'but be sure to make it clear it was the Oval – it couldn't have happened at Lord's!'

For years I was also a football devotee and a very partisan follower of West Ham United. I actually saw the first Cup Final at Wembley Stadium when 'our' team played Bolton Wanderers. Alan, just back from China where he'd been stationed with the Royal Navy, managed to get seats and he, Stuart and I were already in our places when the crowds broke through the barriers in their hundreds. But it all seemed so good humoured. The only policeman really in evidence was mounted on a white horse, constantly clearing the pitch, so that play could be resumed. I've said I was partisan. My team lost and at least one very unhappy fan felt the game should have been replayed, which view was not shared by the jubilant Bolton supporters!

At school I kept a press-cutting book about the fortunes of West Ham. Mother sent me the local newspaper each week so that I could follow their progress. I particularly admired Sid Puddefoot, the great centre-forward not only for West Ham, but for England, and remember still the trembling excitement with which I once took a snapshot of him for my album and the sleepless nights which followed, in case it didn't come out.

Years and years later, about 1937, when I was making a personal appearance at a showing of *Victoria the Great* in Blackpool, my hotel porter told me a Mr Puddefoot was downstairs and would very much like to see me.

It was Sid, wondering whether I would remember him. As if I'd forget one of my greatest heroes!

We lived, in those faraway childhood days, at Forest Gate, long before it became swallowed up in London's urban sprawl. Our house faced West Ham Park; we were within easy reach of Wanstead Park, Wanstead Flats and not too far from Epping Forest itself. It was real Essex countryside, but within easy reach of the docks. Most of our neighbours were the wives of other sea-captains, chief-engineers and so on. Like my mother they were often left alone.

But the Neagles were a very closely-knit family and Aunt Alice and Uncle Edgar and their families also lived at Forest Gate. My cousins were my close friends.

Mother had so much to do, with the three children to bring up and the innumerable practical problems with a husband away on long voyages to the other side of the world. Father's leave periods were short but his home-comings are amongst my happiest childhood memories. Somehow mother always managed to remain gentle and helpful to everyone – even undertaking the honorary secretarial post for the British and Foreign Sailors Society, with its Seaman's Home in the East India Dock Road.

It was in this neighbourhood the Neagles had lived. Helping other people had been ingrained in the family from an early age. She and her three sisters, Alice, Kate and Nellie, 'Auntie Bill' to the family, together with two brothers, Arthur and Edgar, had been brought up in a house next to one occupied by the Cowley Fathers, a group of young Oxford graduates, members of an Anglican Order, who had dedicated their lives to caring for the poor. The Fathers found the atmosphere of my grandparents' home congenial and were in and out frequently. There was, I suppose, an affinity, because my mother's generation, particularly the girls, were very sincere in their religious beliefs. From them I inherited my own deep and supporting Faith.

Aunt Nellie, in particular, devoted her whole life to others. She had not married and so, my mother not enjoying robust health, and finances being tight, decided her place was with her sister.

As each of us arrived, Auntie was there to take charge of everything.

I really must digress to tell you something about Auntie Bill. She was a great character and could without doubt have made her mark as a pianist – or a teacher of children, whom she adored. She was an indefatigable political worker and as Honorary Secretary for the David Howard Habitation, achieved the distinction of being made a Grand Dame of the Primrose League.

At election times Stuart and I would be called on to deliver leaflets, and attend political meetings – all rather boring to a small girl, I'm afraid. It left me without much interest in politics until some years later when, at boarding school, joining in debates and discussions I came to the conclusion I was a good old-fashioned Liberal! The last election my aunt worked for so prodigiously was supporting Captain (as he then was) Margesson who represented West Ham Upton Division.

We left Forest Gate in 1923 to live at Holland Park. From this time on my aunt more than devoted her life to us – she was dedicated. However, she managed between many chores to pursue her favourite hobbies of studying genealogical charts and digging into the past to prove that the Neagles had not always been hard up and that noble blood flowed in their veins. Before she died she had amassed enough letters and documents to prove both – to her satisfaction.

In the case of prosperity, she unearthed a conveyance of a large sugar plantation in Barbados, worth in these days an immense fortune. Unfortunately, the owner, a retired Naval Officer and predecessor of ours, died intestate, leaving the Estate heavily in debt, with many legal problems to be untangled. Finally the matter was placed in Chancery and the fight continued on behalf of a nephew, John Skillet, a minor. Needless to say after years of litigation there was little left of the supposed great fortune.

I must explain that all this took place more than 150 years ago! But, the old parchment documents, preserved in an ancient iron deed box, make fascinating reading. And last year, visiting Barbados, the Head Archivist kindly spent time looking out for me old records which helped fill in the background.

On the genealogical front, Auntie scored a bull's eye.

Augustus Frederick, Duke of Sussex, sixth son of King George III, was a very handsome, warmhearted gentleman who was much attracted to the opposite sex. When young he travelled extensively and during a visit to Rome fell desperately in love with a Lady Augusta Murray, living there with her mother, Lady Dunmore.

There was no question of an 'affaire'. Marriage or nothing. And so an obliging English Chaplain, to assuage the ladies' conscience, performed the ceremony, with only the young couple present and no witnesses.

The Prince's parents, receiving news of their son's activities, commanded his return to England. Secretly he arranged for his 'wife' to follow and equally secretly set her up in a house in Lower Berkeley Street.

But the time arrived when Lady Augusta was expecting a child. Hastily a marriage was arranged at St George's, Hanover Square, for a Mr Augustus Frederick and a Miss Augusta Murray.

Yet, still the meetings of the couple must remain clandestine – with the arrival of a second child, the whole matter came to a head. The marriage was declared null and void under the Royal Marriages Act and the ceremony at Rome completely ignored. As there were no witnesses, quite simply it hadn't happened. That was the reasoning. In due course there was a divorce which brought the whole situation, so fraught with emotion from the beginning, to an unhappy end.

And so the Duke, who appears to have felt no desire to ally himself with one of the numerous eligible members of Royal families of Europe, led the life of a bachelor with many and varied interests. He was gifted with a fine singing voice, of which he was inordinately proud, widely read and travelled.

A strange hobby was a huge collection of birds. But above all, he took an active interest in politics which as a member of the Royal Family, was not customary. Not only did he make lengthy speeches in the House of Lords, espousing the Liberal Cause, but he travelled throughout the country giving his support to the movement for greater understanding of the working man and his intellectual potential.

Nevertheless there was time for such a virile man to engage in the accepted liaisons of that permissive era. Did not the young Princess Victoria have 'a real affection for her uncles, King William and the Duke of Sussex, but Cumberland she always abhorred probably not for his immorality – *they were all immoral* – but on account of the hatred he felt for her and her mother.'*

Near to Windsor there lived a family named Tranter, owners of an Inn. A pretty daughter used to visit a Mrs Gates at the Castle. Apparently she attracted the eye of the Duke and before long, with a baby imminent, she was hurried to France and placed in trusted, well paid hands. The name given to the baby girl she bore was Lucy Beaufoy. Lucy had an excellent education studying all the subjects then regarded as essential for a well brought up young lady, especially music and art.

In due course she was brought back to England and, at St George's, Hanover Square, married her cousin, Charles Tranter. Two Italian names appear on the certificate as witnesses. St George's, Hanover Square, seems an extraordinary Church for the marriage of a simple country girl to an equally simple country cousin – and gives some credence to the story.

The young couple established themselves in a hostelry at Limehouse, the Britannia Tavern. Limehouse still retained, one supposes, some of the colour and prosperity associated with the days of the East India Company, and when a daughter, Fanny, arrived, she also had the benefit of an education at a boarding school which included languages and the arts of music and painting.

Soon an Edward Skillet Neagle appeared on the scene and the result of their marriage was the six children I've mentioned. So far as my aunt was concerned, her appearance without a

*The Early Court of Queen Victoria – Clare Jerrold – 1912

touch of make-up could have taken her to any film set looking every inch a Hanoverian, so like was she to pictures of George III and his predecessor George I.

In delving into this piece of family history my aunt had naturally discovered that the seven sons of King George III and his Queen Charlotte – themselves parents of fifteen – had been remarkably prolific.

Those resulting from Royal marriages, the son and daughter of the Duke of Sussex by his morganatic alliance with Lady Augusta, and the ten children of the Duke of Clarence by Dorothy Jordan, the actress, before his marriage to the Princess Adelaide of Saxe-Meiningen, are all recorded in the history books.

The many illegitimates, although not recognised, were undoubtedly provided for in their upbringing and certainly in the case of my great-grandmother a substantial dowry was forthcoming, from an unknown source, upon her marriage.

Naturally in their youth, with Victorian morality being what it was, this background was not divulged to the Neagle girls and only in later life did they find various documents which sent them on many an expedition to old church yards, registers, and record offices. On one occasion I drove them – highly sceptical of the whole business. But after my Aunt's death in 1964 I found notes and papers which set me off on a little 'delving' myself and the discovery of some items of interest which added support to the story. The whole thing was obviously the wrong side of the blanket, but even that can be comforting – and warm!

There was never much money at home. Father's first command carried the magnificent salary of £240 a year! For this he was responsible for his ship, its cargo and crew. Money went a lot further then, of course, but there was still little to spare. So we had to be careful. But there was a great thing about maintaining standards. Mother had her 'At Home Day' every first Wednesday, when a pretty lace cloth was spread, tiny sandwiches cut and from 4 p.m. to 5 p.m. visitors were expected and welcomed.

Altogether there was a great 'social' atmosphere about our home.

My aunt's philanthropic and political work constantly filled the house with extremely intelligent and influential people. One of her great interests was the Sunday School at Canning Town which she ran. A patron was Lord Frederick Hamilton, son of the Duke of Abercorn. I recall the day when he brought down his sister, the Marchioness of Blandford, together with the astonishingly beautiful Duchess of Marlborough.

They came to the house for tea after visiting the Sunday School. I can still remember her arrival at our small home wearing the most marvellous costume of sapphire blue velvet, a huge hat trimmed with white ostrich feathers and a sable stole. She was quite stunning.

It was Lord Frederick's influence and interest which changed and directed Stuart's whole life. I think it must have been on this day that Stuart sang at the Canning Town Sunday School. Lord Frederick was greatly impressed. To mother and my aunt he said, 'This boy ought to be singing in one of the big choirs. I'll see what I can do.'

What he did was to get Stuart a voice trial at Westminster Abbey. Unfortunately, I developed chicken-pox which put Stuart in quarantine just long enough for him to miss the vacancy in the choir.

Lord Frederick tried again, and this time Stuart gained his place, as a Child of the Chapels Royal, one of the ten Royal choristers who sang in Buckingham Palace, St James's Palace and, at that time, Marlborough House. Also on special occasions at Westminster Abbey.

It was a wonderful experience for Stuart and, through him, in some ways, for me too.

There were ten choir boys and two deputies. They wore, and still wear, 17th century costumes of scarlet and gold, knee breeches and little white neck ruffs. At that time they had their own school out at Streatham in a big early Victorian house where they lived as weekly boarders. Their time was divided between orthodox schooling and music, with the emphasis naturally on music. In Stuart's day the public was permitted to attend Evensong at the Chapel of St James's Palace, and if Stuart was singing the solo we would sometimes go to hear him.

I remember particularly going to St James's on the occasion of the wedding of Prince Arthur, son of the Duke of Connaught, to H.R.H. the Duchess of Fife. We couldn't go to the actual ceremony but waited outside to see the wedding party emerge. Then we *were* allowed in to see the decorations. I was even allowed to sit on the little gilt chair where Queen Mary had sat!

I remember looking round the chapel with eyes like saucers. And I was to remember vividly how that little chapel looked, all decked out for a Royal wedding, when I stood at a faithful film studio reproduction of its altar many years later, as Queen Victoria, plighting her troth to her beloved Albert.

Lord Frederick remained a kind and helpful friend to our family for some years. It was always a happy time when he came to Forest Gate. He was a great teller of stories. One which I've always remembered concerns Sir Edwin Landseer, a close friend of his parents. His mother called at Landseer's St John's Wood home one day and found him in the garden high on a ladder, working on a mass of clay. Turning, she was alarmed to find a full-grown lion on the lawn. Landseer was modelling the lions for Nelson's Column in Trafalgar Square and, as he always preferred working from 'live' models, he had arranged with the zoo to provide him with an elderly, quite harmless creature which had arrived in a furniture van!

As the Duchess didn't know the animal was harmless and hadn't seen the accompanying attendants, her alarm was understandable.

It was shortly before Stuart joined the Chapels Royal that Alan was apprenticed to the sea, the only profession he had ever wished to follow.

As the ship – the *S.S. Indrapura* – sailed out of the London Docks I'm sure I thought my heart would break. I'd been Alan's 'baby' sister, doted on and, I fear, spoiled. Alan's friends had filled the house with laughter and noise when after football on Saturdays they'd poured in for sausages and mash, or fried eggs and bacon. Sometimes looking at a photograph of that Football Club Group I am saddened to realise that so few of them (amongst them, Alan) survived the Great War.

Although father was a sea-captain, in fact he didn't come from the real sea-faring side of my family. It was the Neagles and Skillets who had sea-going connections at least as far back as the 18th century. Then one of them worked alongside Peter the Great when the Tzar was apprenticed at the Dock-yards as a young man, to learn English ship-building.

Great-grandfather Neagle commanded a ship under sail. He came to London from Ireland and retiring from the sea was connected with the East India Docks in the early 1800s, just about the time the Irish dropped the 'e' from the name. He kept it. This sometimes causes confusion. I'm still called 'Nagle' in Ireland and America but 'Neagle' in England.

Father came from farming stock in Fife. His father had joined the Police Force, later coming to South Arundel where he rose to the rank of Superintendent for West Sussex. Nothing much was said about it at home, but I suspect that the mixture of stern police discipline, by a father widowered and left with the care of six children under twelve, cannot have engendered a happy atmosphere. All of them left home young, even my aunts, which was unusual in that generation.

Two of the boys joined the army and two, including my father, 'ran away to sea' in the approved romantic fashion. Following the Neagle tradition my Uncle Arthur had also gone to sea and it was he who brought the slightly lost-and-lonely young Robertson home on leave one day.

It must have been a happy experience for father to move into the serene and closely-integrated home that grandmother had made for her own brood. I don't know how soon he determined to make the connection permanent, but the moment he sat, and passed, his Mate's ticket and moved from the Lower to the Upper Deck, he proposed to mother – and that's where my story really began!

Because his family was so scattered I didn't get to know my Robertson cousins for quite a long time, or much about the family at all, but I do know that father was always very proud of the fact that the Robertsons were a senior clan of Clan Donnachaidh. Malcolm, King of the Scots, was himself a Robertson, and the family had the (unenviable) honour of fighting on the right hand of Prince Charles Edward at the Battle of Culloden.

All of which, come to think of it, makes me a somewhat odd candidate for the critics' 'English Rose'.

Chapter Four

MY FIRST public appearance as a dancer was in Newcastle. My stage was a grey-flagged pavement, my music provided by a barrel-organ, and my appreciative audience a crowd of pop-eyed local children. My performance ended abruptly when mother found me. I'd apparently been missing for hours and she was frantic with worry. She was crosser with me then than I ever saw her before or after, from sheer relief at finding me intact.

After that, whenever I was likely to wander off in strange towns, my name and address were firmly pinned to my coat, with a directive to whoever found me to return me, like a lost parcel.

We quite often did go to strange towns, mother and I, in my early childhood. Always ports, because these journeys were to visit father while he was taking on cargo before a voyage. We usually stayed in a handy boarding-house and visited him on board his ship. Occasionally we even took a little trip with him. I found these visits very reassuring, as well as exciting.

I was almost sick with excitement when he came on leave. He was such an interesting man, and always had the time, patience and knowledge to answer my questions. I once asked him why he 'knew everything'. He laughed, and explained that while at sea the Captain of a ship was never invaded in his quarters by anyone, except by specific invitation. This meant he had hours of solitude to fill. Some Captains took up hobbies, like wood-carving. Father read, widely and intelligently, and stored away facts and impressions as a squirrel stores nuts.

From age five I danced to Aunt Bill's accompaniment. Then mother discovered that some friends were sending their small girls to formal dancing classes. With the family conviction that if you are going to do anything at all, you had better do it properly, she sent me along with them to Miss Dillon's studio, just off Baker Street. Very soon I was having once-a-week ballet lessons, too, with Judith Espinosa.

I was in my seventh heaven. I worked far harder at Miss Dillon's than I did at the little school I attended at Forest Gate, with the result that one day when we arrived for class Miss Dillon told my mother that the previous week she had had a visitor representing Mr J. B. Fagan and Mr C. B. Cochran. They were planning to present four weeks of matinees of Nathaniel Hawthorne Legends under the title *The Wonder Tales*, at the Ambassador's Theatre, Cambridge Circus. They wanted eight little 'Wonder Children' to dance in *Pandora, or the Wonder Box* and *Midas, or the Golden Touch*. Marjorie Robertson had been selected as one of the desirable eight.

Mother was nonplussed. Father, still the decision-maker in the family despite his long absences, was away; but mother had a strong suspicion that he would not approve. In the end she sought the advice of our doctor, who knew me well. He took one look at me and told mother that I would probably be ill with disappointment if I was not allowed to take part!

I was by no means unfamiliar with the professional theatre (from the *wrong* side of the footlights). All mother's family loved it – as spectators – especially the musical side. Among many other stars of the day I'd already seen Adeline Genée and Pavlova dance (every last fluttering wing-feather of Pavlova's immortal Dying Swan lives with me still). To get on to the *right* side of those footlights seemed to me a dazzling prospect.

The Borough Theatre, Stratford, attracted all the great players. About this time, I also saw Beerbohm Tree, George Alexander, Julia Nielsen, Fred Terry and many others, and my resolution strengthened with every theatre visit.

Later, when I was away at school, mother met me off the train at St Pancras with the exciting news that she had tickets for the Royal Albert Hall. That afternoon we heard John McCormack sing.

Mother must have been sorely pressed to have paid for tickets, but she was determined I should see and hear the great artistes.

I'm sure all this did much to increase my desire and when she had taken me to see Pavlova dance, I knew then I must become a great dancer. However, it takes more than desire and determination to do that and I'm afraid the wherewithal was not there.

Those four weeks at the Ambassador's in *Wonder Tales* were among the happiest in my happy childhood. At the end of them I was unshakably stage-struck and set on my course.

Shortly afterwards father arrived home. Almost the first thing he saw was my small attaché case in which I carried my dancing shoes. It bore a large, proud label: *Marjorie Robertson, Child Actress and Dancer.* Father was not amused. Just as mother had suspected, he didn't think he wanted his little girl to go on the stage.

There were family conferences after I had gone to bed, and the upshot was a decision to send me away to boarding school. Not, I am sure, as a punishment. More likely they thought the bracing atmosphere of a good girls' school, lots of sport and the friendship of sensible, ordinary girls might divert my attention from undesirable ambitions.

There was a little more money to spare now. Father was climbing the seniority ladder. Alan, having been made a midshipman RNR at the outbreak of war, was soon to be commissioned to the Royal Navy serving in destroyers and later submarines. Stuart, though still at the Royal College of Music, was soon singing professionally. He was to become the youngest vicar choral ever appointed to the choir of St Paul's Cathedral.

I was not a bit averse to the idea of going away to school, much as I loved my home. Although I had been brought up mainly on the classical novel, I'd enjoyed my Angela Brazil to the full and no doubt like other girls the idea of boarding school struck me as romantic and exciting. So I went off quite cheerfully to St Albans High School for Girls.

There could have been no happier choice. I fitted in immediately, like a hand into a glove. St Albans was a big day school with a small number of boarders divided into three Houses.

I have frequently returned over the years and though the school has doubled in size it seems hardly changed at all in other ways. A matter of months ago I opened a beautiful new Assembly Hall. Sitting on the platform, looking down on the rows of blazered girls, I felt they could just as easily have fitted into my 'year'.

It was, and still is, run by a Church of England Public School Trust, very much under the direction and influence of the Lord Bishop, the Dean, and the Board of Governors who took a strong personal interest – Governorships passing down from father to son.

There was a strong religious training which echoed my own family tradition. We attended services each Sunday in the Abbey; something I have always been grateful for. There was strong, though sensible, discipline too, which I liked. It gave me a sense of security. Reasonable rules and regulations have never worried me and I firmly believe that most children are happier if they are given clear guidance which enables them to distinguish between right and wrong; some yard-stick by which to measure their own life's decisions.

Looking back, St Albans provided an extraordinarily liberal education in every way. Many girls I knew went on to do remarkable things in life.

One, Marjorie Duffell, became an eminent architect, working on the redevelopment, designing and rebuilding of the much-blitzed north-east coast of England after World War II. Another, Sophie Lieck, became a barrister, a rare career for women in those days. A third, Head Girl in my time, Anna Glover, was the first woman to sit on the Army Medical Council in World War II, with the rank of Colonel.

At that time there was an unusually high entry into the Oxbridge Universities, too, on both the Classical and Scientific sides.

To my joy there was an equally strong emphasis on sport, and the team spirit. I played tennis with Kay Stammers, who was to become one of Great Britain's top tennis stars. We were, rather unusually, a cricket school too. It was the first opportunity I had to play in a full team, at any game, and I won both my cricket and netball colours. In fact I was a member of the First Cricket XI during my very first term.

Which leaves hanging that question-mark about my lack of confidence in myself in the theatre.

I don't like self-analysis, particularly with regard to public performance, but *Stand up and Sing* was such an experience I felt I must run it to earth, and reluctantly concluded that the explanation lay partly in the feeling of inferiority to Stuart's glorious voice, partly in the awe inspired by Aunt Nellie's intellectual colleagues, and partly in my father's not wanting me to go on the stage. Throughout much of my career I was the victim of this only half-understood conflict between love of my family and desire to please them; and my instinctive drive towards the theatre.

Mother died without ever seeing me act, or even dance, professionally, except in *Wonder Tales*. Always fragile, she was, I believe, shocked into a debilitating illness by my father's premature retirement after a massive heart-attack in 1924 and all the problems which followed it. From the day she died Aunt Nellie abandoned her many Good Causes to take care of me and keep me fit.

I have a great admiration for the way youngsters in the theatre fend for themselves today. My aunt saved me all the tiresome daily routine of shopping and cooking whilst I was working at pressure.

She lived with me (and later 'us' – Herbert and myself) until her death, ten years ago.

After I left school the question of earning a living arose. Despite St Albans (where I briefly flirted with the idea of becoming a missionary!) I was still set on a stage career. My parents were ever reluctant.

We compromised. At school I had continued to have dancing lessons from a teacher who came to us from 'Mrs Wordsworth's'. Mrs Wordsworth, a formidable old lady, was alleged to have taught Queen Victoria's children to dance. Now she was the Director of a Training College for teachers of dancing and gymnastics. My parents felt that teaching was an acceptable occupation, and teaching dancing and gymnastics would give me an outlet for my obsession.

We did every possible kind of dancing, including a Highland Fling which I was later to use in Cabaret. I learned to fence (which proved useful when I made a film about Peg Woffington, the volatile Irish actress). Leon Bertrand, the celebrated fencing master, arranged the duel for Jack Hawkins and me, and I was glad I knew the rudiments of fencing.

The school was in South Kensington. I travelled there from Forest Gate every day. It was a hard, long day. We had a weekly children's class at which the students, in preparation for their later work in schools, acted as teachers. That was the beginning of the realisation that teaching was not for me. I simply hadn't the patience. I wanted to dance *myself*.

We were also sent out as demonstrators in schools. I remember going to Queen's College, in Harley Street. And there was a weekly dancing class in the Warncliffe Rooms. For the outside classes we students wore neat black dresses and had to wear our long hair tied back, presumably in a desperate effort to add some years to our pathetically obvious few.

I soon grew to hate the whole thing; and to grow desperately tired about this time. Alan had decided to retire from the Royal Navy. He joined Uncle Arthur Neagle, a ship's broker in the City. Stuart, still living at home, was doing a great deal of professional singing, much of it at the Albert Hall and Queen's Hall as well as at St Paul's and around the country. It was then the decision was made to move from Forest Gate to a more central area of London for everyone's convenience.

The house we leased in 1923 at Holland Park was a *six-storey* house. Poor mother! Goodness knows how she coped, increasingly frail as she was with the passing years and the load of responsibility and anxiety she carried, though we did have the help of a maid, and of course Auntie Bill was a tower of strength, and the rest of the aunts rallied round when they could.

I suppose the move must have eased my travelling problems, but I still felt desperately tired – except, oddly enough, when Alan and his friends invited me to go dancing with them in the evening *after* the day's work! I also developed alarming symptons of nervous indigestion. It is obvious now that the tiredness, and the indigestion, were beginning to show.

I must have looked pretty awful for Louisa, the maid, was mournfully convinced that I was 'going into a decline'.

With my father's illness and a sudden drastic reduction of finances, it was decided we must take in a lodger. There was plenty of room in the big house. Poor, delicate Mother, a beautiful needlewoman who had always made most of the clothes for herself, Auntie and me, was now making curtains and chair covers. We were fortunate in finding a charming young Scotsman, in Chambers at the Temple. He had a bedroom and sitting-room, with service of course, but only one meal, breakfast. This was prepared by either my Aunt or myself. Apart from an occasional game of chess with my father, I don't remember seeing him. He rose to high legal office in Scotland. I hope my eggs and bacon helped sustain him in the early days of his legal profession.

The term ended at Wordsworth's and we went down for the summer to Aunt Alice's house at Westcliff-on-Sea. To my enormous relief, after Westcliff it was decided that I shouldn't return to Wordsworth's. Instead I should stay at home and help run the big new house.

I didn't enjoy staying at home at all. I'm not particularly domesticated and found little creative satisfaction in dusting, polishing and cooking breakfast bacon for the boys. I hope my boredom didn't show. Mother and Auntie certainly needed all the help they could get at the time. But I had time to queue up for the gallery to see some of the greats of the theatre – Sybil Thorndike's St Joan – Edith Evans at the Lyric, Hammersmith.

Then, with father at home after his heart-attack which had forced him to retire, and his income reduced to a shadow of its former self, I decided I *must* earn some money. Teaching dancing was all I could do, so I cashed in on the ballroom dancing boom of the 'twenties and started to give occasional lessons at a big London hotel. Perhaps, I thought optimistically, I would enjoy teaching adults more than children.

I didn't. I still loved to dance with Alan and his friends, but trying to teach adults, at ten shillings a time, was heavy going. But (with a superb partner) I did have the thrill of reaching the finals in the Star Ballroom Championships in waltz, foxtrot *and* tango!

Also, I had one brief happy week which threw the whole of this desolate period into even greater relief when a friend of Stuart's, who was a member of the Stock Exchange, suggested I joined the cast of one of their famous annual amateur shows at the Scala Theatre. They were presenting *The Geisha* that year. I can still remember the first night of that production more clearly than many of my professional first nights. If I shut my eyes I can still smell the grease-paint, hear the sound of the orchestra tuning-up, the swish of the curtain, the rustle of the audience.

After it was over, I was left more stage-struck then ever, and life seemed even less satisfactory.

In the end father realised that things were not working out for me as they should. He knew why, too, and with his usual good sense, and sense of justice, decided it was no use any longer hoping I would 'grow out of it'.

'Well,' he said at last, 'you'll have to be self-supporting now and I know it's the stage you want. You'd better try your hand at it.'

I'm sure I was out of the room before he had finished talking. But I ran back to give him a quick hug of gratitude.

Chapter Five

As soon as father agreed to my doing stage work, I went back to my old friend Miss Dillon like a homing-pigeon, and began to attend her theatrical dancing classes. After a short time she sent me for my first audition. Strangely enough it was for the chorus of the tour of *No, No, Nanette*, the show in which I most recently starred at Drury Lane! I was turned down. It would have been surprising had I not been.

'Never mind, dear, it was good experience,' Miss Dillon consoled me, and sent me off again, to see Jack Hulbert who was then running The Little Revue at the Little Theatre. He wanted only six girls. I made it into the final sixteen, and felt this was a small step forward.

Then Miss Dillon heard that the French impresario, André Charlot, was casting for one of his famous revues and along I went. My heart sank when I saw the vast numbers of hopefuls already queueing up. They all seemed to know each other, and chattered excitedly. Several, recognising me as a newcomer, advised me not to admit my lack of experience.

I stood in line, feverishly muttering to myself: 'Muriel Durelle . . . Muriel Durelle . . .' the name I'd decided to use as a professional disguise.

Carrie Graham, the ballet mistress, came on-stage and began to take particulars. The other girls cheerfully rattled off their names and previous experience.

At last she reached me. 'And your name is . . . ?' she asked, without looking up.

'Mu . . . Mum . . . Mu . . . Mmmmm . . . arjorie Robertson,' I ended with a rush. She looked up at that. 'And what else have you done?' she inquired gently.

'Nu . . . nu . . . nothing . . .'

She laughed but not unkindly. 'You needn't really have told me that,' she chuckled. 'It's written all over you. Oh, don't worry, dear,' she added, seeing my distress. 'We all have to start somewhere.'

Half an hour later I was standing outside the stage door in a state of utter bliss. I was in! I had a job in the chorus of André Charlot's revival of *Bubbly*. It exactly described how I felt!

And so my first really professional appearance on stage, discounting the *Wonder Tales,* was at the Duke of York's Theatre. Though I don't remember the first night of *Bubbly* as well as that of *The Geisha*, during rehearsals I still clearly remember receiving my first half-week's pay: thirty-two shillings. I remember sending across the road to a little restaurant opposite, as all the girls did, for steak and chips to eat in the dressing-room during rehearsals. Oh, it was a wonderful feeling. I felt independent, I felt a Pro, I felt sophisticated and worldly and madly happy. I felt I had arrived.

Bubbly ran for only six weeks in London. Then we went on tour. Another thrill: my first experience of living in theatrical digs, and an extension of my feeling of independence. In those days theatrical digs were very specialised. The landladies didn't take anyone *but* theatre people. They varied in quality, naturally, but the good ones were *very* good. Some stars chose to live in them, rather than hotels, because they understood and catered for the problems of theatre people.

Some landladies had been on the stage themselves, or been in some way connected with it, perhaps as Dressers. Those in the top bracket often had great dignity and a great reputation in the profession. They knew we would not be arriving home until after midnight sometimes; that we would be hungry and, despite a long hard evening's work, disinclined to sleep until our over-stimulated nerves had relaxed.

I remember best of all the big coal fires which always seemed to be waiting for us, and our sitting round them, sipping steaming cups of tea, or cocoa, and talking over the evening's show; comparing Tuesday's audience with Monday's and wondering why they laughed some nights more than others.

With the increased speed of travel and the sad shrinking in the numbers of theatrical tours, digs like these have dwindled to a tiny handful. I'm glad I had a chance to enjoy them while they existed.

I worked in two more superbly-staged Charlot Revues, with stars such as Gertrude Lawrence, Bea Lillie, Jessie Matthews, Jack Buchanan, Cyril Ritchard and Edmund Gwenn. Just watching them was marvellous training.

I was deeply disappointed when I had to drop out of the second Charlot tour because it was becoming obvious that mother was going rapidly downhill, and I shouldn't be too far from home.

Instead, I joined a short run of Dion Titheridge's Revue, *Tricks*, and it was from this that I went into a late-night Cochran Cabaret called *Supper Time* in the Grill Room of the Trocadero Restaurant. *Supper Time* was later to merge into *Merry-go-Round,* and *Merry-go-Round* into *Champagne Time.* Altogether I spent about three years in Cabaret at the Troc. These were miniature revues, in true Cochran style, but just doing midnight Cabaret was no longer enough. I really had the bit between my teeth now, and kicking my heels all day, waiting for my nightly 10.30 p.m. journey to work soon made me restless again. Apart from that, if I could get more work I could be earning more and that would be useful. Money was pretty tight at home.

Because mother was so unwell I couldn't take touring

work, but by great good luck, in March 1926 I was offered a stand-by job at Drury Lane for the chorus of *Rose-Marie*. This meant being a sort of understudy, capable of picking up the work of any girl who was ill, or away, so I had a lot of rehearsing to keep me busy, even though I only occasionally appeared on-stage. For the moment it was a perfect solution. Apart from anything else I was far too worried about mother, especially after she was taken into hospital and we all knew that she was unlikely ever to come out again.

The day I went 'on' for the first time I dashed to the Westminster Hospital after the matinee. Mother's condition was obviously worse. When father and Stuart came together to meet me that Saturday night it wasn't necessary for them to tell me in words that mother had died. We all went home together silently, to a silent home.

What now? Did I leave the theatre to become the 'maternal' pivot of the family? Aunt Bill soon sorted that question out. No doubt my year at home had convinced her that I would never be a practical housewife. Much better for me, the whole family agreed, to do the job I knew and loved, and leave the domestic side of things to her. So she quietly took over the reins, and ran my home-life for me, contentedly and efficiently, for the next twenty-five years.

Alan accepted a post which took him to South Africa and we were not to meet again for twenty-two years. Stuart, too, was away more and more. Shortly after mother's death he went to Australia to accompany Dame Nellie Melba, at her own request, on her really-and-truly final Farewell Tour.

An echo of this tour occurred during the war when Stuart was a Lieutenant Commander in the Canadian Navy and C.O. of an extraordinarily good Service revue *Meet The Navy* drawn from Canadian serving naval personnel.

The show played at the London Hippodrome, where I got my first big stage chance with Jack Buchanan in *Stand*

Above : Me, aged eighteen months.
Below : The Neagle family : *(Standing, left to right)* Uncle Edgar Neagle, Aunt Nellie Neagle, Uncle Arthur Neagle. *(Sitting, left to right)* My mother (Mrs Florence Robertson), Aunt Alice (Mrs Dudley Stuart), Grandfather Edward Neagle and Aunt Kate (Mrs Arthur Terry).

Top left: The tavern owned by Charles Tranter and his wife Lucy Beaufoy Tranter.

Top right: Marriage certificate of Charles and Lucy Beaufoy Tranter at St George, Hanover Square, 1834.

Bottom left: My father.

Bottom centre: The sailing ship, *Trossacks*, in which my father made his first voyage.

Bottom right: My home at Upton Lane, Forest Gate. I am the little girl with my mother at the upstairs window and my brother, Stuart, is at the gate.

Top left: My first public appearance! A photograph of the Robertson family with mother, father, Alan and Stuart.

Top right: My grandparents Robertson with three of their sons. My father is the little boy on the left and his brothers are Alfred and James.

Bottom: The Neagle sisters: Mrs Robertson (my mother), Aunt Nellie Neagle, Aunt Kate (Mrs Terry) and Aunt Alice (Mrs Stuart).

Top left: With my cousin, May Stuart, at a fancy dress party at the Stratford Town Hall.
Top right: Stuart as a Child of the Chapels Royal, the choristers who sing at the chapels of Buckingham Palace and St James's Palace.
Bottom left: My brother, Lt Alan Robertson R.N., 1918.
Bottom right: Stuart – taken when he accompanied Dame Nellie Melba on her last concert tour of Australia, 1927.

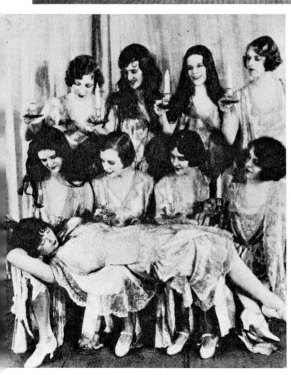

Tel. Algonquin 4485

NATIONA
Press Clipping
Inc.
31 East 17th S
NEW YORK C

FROM

Public Ledger
PHILADELPHIA

ENGLAND'S
"SUPER-CHORUS
GIRL": MARJORIE
ROBERTSON
who, according to
Charles B. Cochran,
the "British Zieg-
feld," is the glori-
fication of the type
he wants for his
next American pro-
duction, "Wake Up
and Dream"
© E. O. Hoppe

Top: Scene from *The Desert Song,* presented at the Drury Lane Theatre, 1927, starring Edith Day. I am sixth from the left, still Marjorie Robertson.
Bottom left: Jessie Matthews with a bevy of Cochran Young Ladies in *Wake Up and Dream:* I am in the back row, top right. *(The Mander & Mitchenson Theatre Collection).*
Bottom right: An American press clipping before *Wake Up and Dream* opened in New York in 1930.

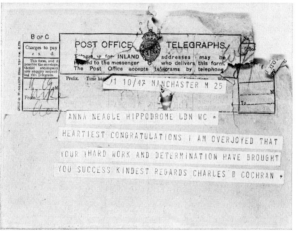

Top: Scene from the dress rehearsal of *Wake Up and Dream* with Mr Charles B. Cochran. I am third from the left and Oliver Messel, the designer of the production, is second from the right.
Centre: Congratulatory message from 'Cocky' after the opening performance of *Stand Up and Sing.*
Below left: With Jack Buchanan in *Stand Up and Sing* at the London Hippodrome.
Below right: With Jack Buchanan in a scene from *Goodnight Vienna* (1932), my first major film role.
Next page: The dress that shocked! In *The Little Damozel,* 1933.

Top: With Herbert and Fernand Gravet in the film production of Noël Coward's *Bitter Sweet,* 1933.

Centre: Noël Coward with his three original Sari Lindens, Peggy Wood *(right),* who created the role in London, Evelyn Laye *(left),* who played it in New York, and myself.

Below: As Nell Gwyn, 1934. *Nell Gwyn,* produced and directed by Herbert, was the first film banned in the United States under the Purity Code.

up and Sing and where Herbert first saw me perform. King George VI and Queen Elizabeth came to see *Meet The Navy* and Stuart, as C.O., had to greet them.

The Queen looked at Stuart and said: 'We've met before.'

'Yes, Ma'am,' replied Stuart.

'Where?' asked the Queen.

'At Canberra, Ma'am, when I was singing with Dame Nellie Melba.'

'Oh, yes – of course, I remember,' she said. Stuart always marvelled that she should have remembered so brief a meeting, after so many years.

During my time in *Rose-Marie*, I gained my full place in the chorus, and almost automatically went into the next Drury Lane show: *The Desert Song*, starring wonderful Edith Day. In fact, at one point I was rehearsing *Desert Song* in the mornings, playing *Rose-Marie* some afternoons and every evening, then going straight on to the midnight Cabaret at the Troc. Even I could hardly cram more theatre into one day!

In *Desert Song*, we had a show-stopping number, dressed as young *poilus* in the smart military uniform of the French Foreign Legion. Everything seemed very rosy indeed.

I left the *Desert Song* for another stand-by chorus job, this time in C. B. Cochran's London Pavilion show *One Damn Thing After Another*. (Odd how the titles of ''twenties' shows so often seemed to reflect what was actually happening in my private life!)

One Damn Thing After Another was my first Cochran theatre show and I realise now that the changeover from *Desert Song*, excellent though that show was, was a great piece of luck for me. It had a wonderful cast. The West End seems, in hindsight, to have been full of highly talented and thoroughly professional artistes at that time – perhaps because so many, like myself, spent many years as apprentices in the humbler reaches of the

49

chorus. My heart bleeds for the overnight stars of the television age, who find themselves catapulted into the limelight long before they are ready to sustain it.

At the London Pavilion there were, among others, Douglas Byng to make the audience laugh, Sonnie Hale and Jessie Matthews to sing, and to dance divinely. She made a terrific impact. I'd worked with her before, of course, and admired her tremendously. If anyone had a 'something' about her, it was Jessie. She was elfin, with enormous brown eyes. She had other, more obvious, qualities too. Like Jack Buchanan, when she danced she gave a new meaning to the word 'legs'. Hers were wonderfully long, beautifully shaped and kicked higher, more gracefully, than any others I have ever seen. She had an almost feline agility. Without apparent effort she could rise from the floor to a full standing position in one lovely sinuous movement. And I think what endeared her to me was that she *worked* so hard.

I was offered second-understudy to Jessie, which was a rather frightening responsibility. It was the second opportunity I'd had to understudy a lead. I'd been offered second-understudy to the second lead in *Rose-Marie* but had backed away from that like a frightened rabbit! This time I felt that if I was ever to get anywhere except the chorus I must be a little braver. One of the numbers I had to rehearse was the very popular *My Heart Stood Still*, not at all an easy one to sing (I didn't make much of it). Luckily I was never put to the test before an audience, otherwise I might never even have contemplated Jack's invitation to join *Stand up and Sing*.

Chapter Six

ONE *Damn Thing After Another* was followed by what is possibly still the finest revue ever staged, Noël Coward's *This Year of Grace*. C. B. Cochran presented it, and it was now that he had the bright idea of dropping the label 'chorus girl' and retitling us 'Young Ladies'. We found this embarrassing at first, but it caught on so fast, and singled us out so dramatically that after a while we began to wear the title with pride, and a certain possessive jealousy.

The book and songs (music and lyrics) and the direction of *This Year of Grace* were all Noël's. Jessie starred again, with Sonnie Hale, Maisie Gay, and the Viennese dancer Tilly Losch. It was a huge, wonderful cast.

I have one particularly vivid memory of rehearsals. We, the chorus, were sitting about at the back of the cold rehearsal room in Poland Street waiting to be called, while Sonnie was wrestling with one of the numbers (now a classic of its kind) *Dance, Little Lady*. He was obviously unhappy about it. The rhythm was extremely new at the time and he couldn't 'get it'. We all felt for him. We could sense that not only the words, but the rhythm of the music were potentially very exciting, but none of us understood it. We could see, too, that Noël was becoming increasingly restless and agitated.

Presently Sonnie stopped, and threw up his hands. 'Noël, I'm sorry. I just can't get the hang of this at all . . .'

Noël bounded forward. 'Now come along, dear boy . . . Let me show you. Let me show you . . .'

What followed was one of the most electrifying things I've ever seen in the theatre.

Here really was The Master at work.

> 'Dance . . . dance . . . *dance* little lady
> Youth is fleeting . . .'

Noël was very young and slim, his brilliance almost lighting up that bare, drab room, his voice, hands and feet beating out this (to us) extraordinary new rhythm. I never saw him do anything at a performance which left such a vivid and lasting impression.

There were two other very fine American speciality dancers in the show: Jack Holland and Jean Barry. After the Dress Rehearsal Jack Holland approached me and asked whether I'd like to understudy Jean. Once again, he hadn't noticed me until I was made-up, costumed, and theatrically lit. Although I was never called on to take Jean's place, rehearsing with Jack was an invaluable experience.

When we opened in London, after a smash-hit tour, it was to a sensational welcome; and it was now that I began to find life opening out in other ways.

C. B. Cochran, apart from being a brilliant impresario, took a kindly interest in all his artists, but especially 'his girls'. His discipline was strict, and he noticed everything. I still have some of the little notes he used to send us whenever we transgressed some theatre rule such as arriving late. On one occasion when I missed two entrances within a few days he expressed himself 'terribly hurt by this neglect of your work' – and he doubled my fine for the second transgression! But he never forgot the encouraging word, either; and there were always flowers for us in the dressing-room on first nights, and a word of thanks from him when the show was successfully over, as there was from Noël, too.

I was particularly touched a little later when I went to America for the first time. C.B. knew, amongst other things, the home-backgrounds of all the girls and a few weeks before we sailed he had a quiet word with me.

'Are you all right for money, Marjorie?' he asked.

'Yes, quite all right, thank you.' I was actually earning quite good money now, with the Cabaret and shows – ten pounds a week!

'You don't need a sub?'

I shook my head, and smiled. 'No thank you,' I told him.

During the summer months he used to invite us, two or three at a time, to stay for weekends at the country house he and Mrs Cochran would take for the season. There was tennis, swimming, boating on the river. There were at these house-parties not only people from our own show but American Producers and *entrepreneurs*, and other theatre people, besides politicians, people from the Press and many other walks of life – people who could talk on a wide range of subjects.

Now I found myself more and more included in after-show supper-parties too. I remember once finding myself sitting next to a young Oxford Graduate, whom I'd previously met when visiting Mary Black, an old school friend at Oxford, lecturing me earnestly on the value of the five-day week. This was back in the late 1920's when such an idea was revolutionary – it frankly appalled me! 'But what would people *do* if they only worked five days a week?' I asked. 'Surely they'd be bored on the days they weren't working?' I, of course, loved my work so much I even resented Sunday keeping me away from it! I would willingly have worked seven days a week – which indeed I did, in films, on many occasions.

J. P. W. 'Curly' Mallalieu laughed. 'It's all right for some. How would you like it if you worked on a factory assembly line? No, we must educate people to use their leisure creatively – constructively; to open up their lives to art, music, literature. To take up hobbies, enjoy sport, that sort of thing.'

Now we have the five-day week, with the four, or even three-day week in prospect I often wonder whether he feels satisfied with the way that extra leisure is being used.

We met a lot of bright young aristocratic and attractive socialites at parties too. Though I loved those evenings dancing to the gorgeous sound of the Big Band era, for me, with my simple, frugal background, it wasn't always easy to keep up with the oyster, caviare and champagne atmosphere and especially the expensive and glamorous wardrobes of the girls. I remember when we were invited to the Savoy one night being lent a perfectly heavenly dress by Sheilah Graham, then a Cochran Young Lady. Later she became famous as an American columnist, and even more famous as Scott Fitzgerald's companion. Her sensational autobiography *Beloved Infidel* was made into a very successful film.

I still see her occasionally. Much to the surprise of Herbert, she came to see *Charlie Girl* several times while it was running at the Adelphi. 'You here again?' said Herbert. 'You're supposed to be a sophisticated bitch.' 'Flatterer,' replied Sheilah. The two are great friends!

My life now was settling down into a very interesting and fulfilling routine. We had found a small but comfortable flat in Maida Vale, and begun at last to turn it into a real home. We had been living in so-called 'Private Hotels' in Bayswater and Bloomsbury since leaving Holland Park after my mother's death. Stuart had married upon his return home from Australia. Father, his health improved, was working again for the New Zealand Shipping Company.

Even before I went to America my ambition had begun to put out small, tentative shoots. Round about the time of the changeover from *ODTAA* to *This Year of Grace* I was dancing one night with John Paddy Carstairs, son of Nelson Keys. John Paddy was 'in films' as a very junior Assistant Director.

'Why don't you come down to Cricklewood for crowd work?' he suggested. 'You'd like to be in films, wouldn't you?'

'Who wouldn't!'

'Well then – I think you'd photograph well. Herbert Wilcox is filming *The Triumph of the Scarlet Pimpernel* at present. Go and see him.'

I did just that. I remember arriving at the Cricklewood Studios one bleak winter's morning; reporting to the Reception Desk and being told to sit down and wait. The only seat available was in a direct line with the door, which was constantly being opened and shut. I felt myself turning blue as time passed and 'Mr Wilcox won't be long now' became a monotonous refrain.

In fact I saw Mr Wilcox several times, whirling through the Reception Hall to his office, presumably to take important telephone calls from Hollywood. He eventually noticed me. He rang through to ask, 'Who's that girl who looks as though she's freezing to death?'

So at last, shaking as much with cold as nerves for once, I went in to his office only to hear the words which were to become so familiar in the not-too-distant future: 'Well, I'm sorry ... there's nothing at the moment. Send me a photograph and if anything turns up ...'

That night I wrote in my diary: 'Saw Herbert Wilcox today about work in films. Think I'll stick to the chorus.'

Cochran followed the stupendous *This Year of Grace* with *Wake up and Dream* – Jessie and Sonnie, and Tilly Losch again. There were some lovely settings by Oliver Messel (and Rex Whistler, too), and music by Cole Porter.

Again I had the encouraging experience of acting as an understudy for one of Jessie's dances. This time a lovely number with Sonnie Hale: *Looking at You*. They were both, but particularly Jessie, marvellously helpful at rehearsals, just as Jack Holland had been in *This Year of Grace*. Gradually, working with such experts, I was building up and perfecting my own technique. This time I actually did appear when Jessie had a month's leave towards the end of the London run. I didn't exactly set the Thames on fire, but I *did* it.

By now the legend of the beauty and charm, as well as the expertise, of Cochran's 'Young Ladies' had spread like wildfire. When we arrived in Manchester there were our photographs and our names on the posters, our photographs (and vital statistics) in all the newspapers. You could almost see our heads swelling!

By the time we reached New York, the American journalists were waiting for us, too.

It was Christmas Eve, 1929. Too many more experienced writers than I have written eloquently of their first glimpse of the New York skyline for me to want to compete with them. I can only agree that it is a once-in-a-lifetime event almost beyond description, followed, in my case at least, by a great let-down when, almost immediately on landing at Hoboken – not New York! – I found a run-down, shabby suburb of New York quite out of keeping with the fairy-like magic of the tall lighted buildings I had seen from the ship.

I adored New York. There really was a stimulus in the very air we breathed there which I'd never experienced before. Today the pace has become frenetic and the atmosphere polluted. Then it was just exciting.

The very first thing we did on arrival was to rush to the theatre. Not *our* theatre. We were taken that Christmas Eve to see another English musical play at that time taking Broadway by storm. Noël Coward's enchanting *Bitter Sweet*, with Evelyn Laye playing Sari. Even in off-duty hours most of us haunted theatres. We all carried pass-cards printed with the name of the show in which we were appearing ourselves. If there were unoccupied seats in any other theatre, those magical passes allowed us to use them. In this way I saw practically every show of any description in London, and quite a few while we were in New York.

I had already seen *Bitter Sweet* in London, with Peggy Wood as the original Sari, but I wasn't going to miss the chance of seeing Evelyn Laye too. She had been one of my idols ever since I'd seen her in *Madame Pompadour* at Dalys.

We ourselves opened at the Selwyn Theatre on December 31st 1929, and during the run I became friendly with the owner's son, Archie, who took me out on the town in a way which would no longer be possible. Apart from meeting people like Eddie Cantor, the Marx Brothers, and Ruth Etting, the popular singer of *Ten Cents a Dance*, who had only been names, or voices, or shadows on the screen before, we often went downtown to Harlem, late at night, and we frequented speak-easies, those dark little half-accepted drinking places which proliferated during the years of Prohibition. We were a happy company, and we had a ball.

Out of character? Perhaps. But we are none of us, thank goodness, all-of-a-piece.

Odd, unsuspected bits of Anna Neagle were to emerge later, when I was filming, which startled even Marjorie Robertson!

Chapter Seven

IT was that dynamic, stimulating trip to New York which, as I've already described, gave my ambition the extra push it needed, and though the beginning was hard, once I'd made the break-through it all seemed worth-while.

One of the nice things about playing a part, instead of just being in the chorus, was having my own dresser. *Stand up and Sing* was the first time I was to experience this pleasure. 'Louie' came to me then. She was to stay with me until I went to Hollywood at the end of the decade.

She made life so much easier for me: giving me little tips, protecting me from too many visitors, always making sure that my dresses were in perfect condition, that I was ready in good time for my entrances – all without fuss.

After the war her daughter, Maudie, dressed me for a while and used to tell me the old 'bomb story', but about Louie. During a raid everyone in their building was ordered into the cellars. No sooner were they settled than Louie began to scuttle out again. The Air Raid Warden called her back.

'Where d'you think *you're* going?' he demanded.

'Back upstairs,' Louie mumbled. 'I've left my teeth in a glass beside me bed.'

'Come *back*,' the Warden yelled after her. 'What d'you think they're dropping – 'am sandwiches?'

Louie helped me to relax with her competence and her calmness. It's extraordinary how important a good dresser is to an artiste. Apart from Louie and Maudie I've had Helen Hough, who not only dressed me, but took care of some of my correspondence, and Gillie – who saw me through *Charlie Girl* and *No, No, Nanette* – saved me endless worries, was never flustered and always cheerful. I am glad to acknowledge here how much they were appreciated.

Dear Jack Buchanan, if he were here, would endorse what I have been saying because he had for many years a gentleman's gentleman, a unique dresser – valet factotum. I never heard his christian name. He was just Green. Quiet, dignified, discreetly invisible when necessary, but always on hand when wanted. Green knew Jack and Jack knew Green.

Green died only a short time before Jack and as Susie Buchanan, Jack's lovely wife (knowing how ill Jack was) put it, 'Green's gone ahead to see everything is O.K. for Jack!'

I settled down and began to enjoy life. In fact one day I enjoyed life a bit too much. An old friend from chorus days was getting married. I couldn't go to the wedding because it was a matinee day, but agreed to dash round between shows to drink her health.

I did: two glasses of champagne, on an empty stomach. When the time came for me to make my entrance that night I sailed on to the stage with the poise of a seasoned trouper. I danced more gaily, more lightly and more freely than ever before. Until I came to a series of pirouettes . . .

Off-stage Jack caught my arm. 'What's the matter, baby? Are you all right? Are you ill?'

'Oh no,' I replied with a seraphic smile. 'I've just been drinking too much.' And I floated away to my dressing-room.

In the interval there was a knock on the door. Green arrived with a large pot of black coffee and a plate of chicken sandwiches 'compliments of Mr Buchanan, and please see that you eat them all; and would you please see Mr Buchanan at the fall of the curtain.'

It was this, as much as the coffee and sandwiches, that

sobered me. It was like a school summons to see the head-mistress after class.

I turned up as instructed, at the fall of the curtain, and waited for what we later called 'a rocket'. It came.

What did I mean: I'd 'had too much to drink'?

Meekly I explained, half-expecting an indulgent reply. But Jack remained stern.

'Now you make a rule. You *never* drink before going on stage. I have a couple of gin-and-tonics myself when it's over, but *nothing*, ever, before the show.'

I promised, and I've kept that promise; but there was a little echo of my experience not many years ago when I was touring in *Person Unknown*. The young man playing the part of the fiancé of a murdered girl had one very emotional scene. He normally played it extremely well, but with decent restraint. One night I was startled to find he was actually *sobbing*. Rivers of tears flooded down his face. When it was time for him to make his exit, he stayed on-stage, wandering about in a state bordering on hysteria. In the end two other actors managed to manoeuvre him off without (we hoped) the audience realising that something was wrong.

The Stage Director was furious. We were playing in Hull at the time and apparently this young actor had been invited aboard a Russian vessel that afternoon and there had been a good many rounds of vodka!

Joyce, my secretary, went out to get black coffee for *him* on that occasion and the Stage Director, worried about my reaction, asked her not to tell me the truth.

'I expect she's guessed, anyway. She'll understand. But I think you ought to apologise . . .' she added to the culprit, busy repairing his make-up.

He came to my dressing-room after the play ended, looking so sheepish that I couldn't resist telling him my champagne story, and Jack's service, which I hope remained with him.

Stand up and Sing was a great success and both my dance and my voice improved every performance.

And then came my second stroke of luck.

In a few days time Jack was due to commence a film *Goodnight Vienna* but the Producer, Herbert Wilcox, could not find a leading lady. He decided to postpone production and came to the London Hippodrome to tell Jack that Evelyn Laye or Lea Seidl were not available.

A matinee was in progress and Frank Boor, the Manager, suggested that Herbert see the show out and he'd take him round to Jack's dressing-room afterwards.

He looked at the stage – I was dancing and Jack was singing! Yes – *There's Always Tomorrow*. (Perhaps this will enable you to appreciate why I chose to give this title to my book.) Herbert watched for a few minutes then, without waiting for Frank Boor, was in Jack's dressing-room in minutes.

'Here we are searching Europe for our leading lady,' he said, 'and she's right here in your show.'

'You mean Anna Neagle?' asked Jack.

When Herbert told him he did – Jack shook his hand. 'They tell me she won't photograph, old boy,' said Jack. 'Eyes too blue – cheek-bones too high.'

'Yes,' said Herbert, 'they told me that when I asked to see her and was told that you weren't bringing her into town. But now I've seen you together I'll take her – blue eyes and high cheek-bones!"

'I couldn't be happier if you did,' said Jack. 'I'm sure she'll look good and she's extremely hard-working.'

So without a test, which Herbert brushed aside as useless, I found myself in a day or so at Elstree Studios playing the lead to the great Jack Buchanan!

Although I was happy and excited that sunny, frosty early-December morning as I walked up the hill to the Elstree Studios there were still the old flutters of nervousness!

Typical of Herbert's thoughtfulness and kindness was that he always arranged for someone to be at the gate of the studios to meet people arriving for the first time. They would be told exactly where to go, and given a cup of tea or coffee. It was only a small thing, but reassuring out of all proportion to the trouble caused.

In this film I played the part of a flower-shop girl whose lover goes away to war. Herbert arranged for Moyses Stevens, the famous London flower-shop, to do the whole thing and I still have a memento of it. Standing on a table by the window in our sitting-room is the green bowl which was filled with gardenias that morning all those years ago.

Filming all day was hard, demanding work of course and Jack and I were still playing *Stand up and Sing* in the evenings as well. The film *had* to be finished in three weeks to enable us to start the second tour of the play, beginning with a six-week Christmas season at the Empire Theatre, Liverpool.

Jack had to go up ahead of the rest of us on the Monday of Christmas week, to make sure everything was ready for the Dress Rehearsal on Wednesday, so our last scenes together in the film had to be completed by Sunday night, or at latest the small hours of Monday morning.

By midnight we were all beginning to feel the strain. We were making a big scene in a garden-café in Vienna, Jack singing one of the main numbers: *Living in Clover*. The rest of us were sitting around in attitudes of 'relaxed delight', drinking glass after glass of champagne. Although it wasn't champagne of course, it was ginger-ale! We'd had nothing to eat for hours and we were ravenous; but Herbert pressed on until the Sound Man, in despair, called a halt. 'Sorry, Mr Wilcox, we'll just have to have a break and give them something to eat. I'm picking up nothing but tummy-rumbles!'

We came back shortly, fortified by sandwiches, and picked up where we had left off – with one difference. This time the liquid in the glasses *was* champagne. Just enough to give us a lift, not enough to upset our equilibrium. The scene went without a hitch and by 2 a.m. everything connected with Jack was in the can. I still had an odd scene or two to tidy up, mainly close-ups, which kept me busy until Tuesday. When the time came for me to leave, Herbert called me into his office and pointed out that my original agreement had been £150 for three weeks' work (we had signed no formal contract) but that since I had run into a fourth week, and put in a tremendous amount of extra work over the weekend he intended to add fifty pounds to my cheque.

Jack told me a few days later, that Herbert was extremely pleased with the way the picture was coming together, and that he proposed bringing it up to Newcastle for us, and all the *Stand up and Sing* company to see.

It was a Sunday evening. Herbert gave us all an egg-and-bacon supper at the hotel, and when the cinema was officially closed we trooped across to see my first important film.

I had mixed feelings as I watched it. Some parts I thought not too bad; others much better than I expected. Occasionally I squirmed in my seat! On the whole I was not too disappointed, and the reaction of the *Stand up and Sing* company was comforting and encouraging.

Herbert stayed overnight and the next day sent a message to the small hotel in Whitley Bay where I was staying, asking me to have tea with him before he went south.

He told me he was delighted with my work, and the film generally, and he hoped we would work together again. Then he produced a spray of lilies-of-the-valley (one of my favourite flowers) and presented it to me almost shyly. I was very touched.

The making of *Goodnight Vienna* was a happy experience indeed – except for one thing!

Although he did not say a word, I knew Herbert had become very attracted to me – possibly was in love with me. I also knew he had a wife and family and I was not one to disturb domestic happiness.

On April 5th 1932 *Goodnight Vienna* was trade shown in Birmingham, followed by a Press lunch which finished rather late.

Herbert asked me round to his hotel for a cup of tea.

Before he left for London he made an agreement with me for three years.

He also confessed his love for me, but told me it would not be allowed to disturb our working together. But he wanted me to know how he felt.

He was as good as his word. He did not refer to it again and our work continued without embarrassment.

I shall always remember April 5th 1932.

Another date is May 13th 1932.

Wisely, I think, with so much on his mind, Herbert made a point of having one day a week away from all business and production matters. May 13th was one of those days.

He phoned me at home and asked if I would like a day in the country. 'The bluebells are out,' he told me.

I gladly accepted and we drove down to Coldharbour, just beyond Dorking. It was a spot he knew but to me it was new ground. We stopped the car and Lowen, his chauffeur and good friend, unloaded the boot which contained a lunch basket.

We climbed a hill from which we could see the South Downs and a chunk of Surrey and Sussex. A magnificent view.

Lowen laid out our lunch: sandwiches of cold salmon on brown bread and champagne.

Below us in the valley a village cricket match was in progress (the sound of bat hitting ball delayed by the distance), otherwise no sound except that of birds and the occasional plane.

Conversation was unnecessary – there were bluebells in abundance, offset by azaleas and rhododendrons. A moment of sheer bliss.

I realised then that I felt about Herbert as he did about me. As though knowing my thoughts he said: 'Supposing I was free, would you marry me?'

'Yes,' I replied without hesitation.

'That's all I wanted to know,' he told me.

That night he took me to the Hammersmith Theatre where *Stand up and Sing* was playing its last week. We had a drink together with Jack in his dressing-room and then went on to the Embassy Club for supper.

Yes – a day to remember. *May 13th 1932.*

In April 1974 I was engrossed and immersed in writing this book. Looking up press cuttings, photographs and diaries etc. An exhausting process that seemed to drain me. Herbert suddenly appeared and said, 'I've made a lunch date for you on Friday.'

'But I just can't,' I told him, 'the deadline is coming up fast – and a lunch date will shatter my concentration.'

'Do you realise Friday is April 5th and you are lunching with me?' said Herbert.

'Of course,' I answered, 'all this made me forget – where are we going this year?'

'Coldharbour,' replied Herbert, 'a picnic lunch – too early for bluebells but it will do you good to get away for a few hours.'

So on April 5th 1974 we celebrated both April 5th and May 13th!

On our first visit to Coldharbour it was sandwiches of fresh salmon on brown bread and champagne – and a tomato.

This time it was precisely the same – and the sun shone the day long.

Herbert was right. I had for some little time been having difficulty in getting off to sleep, largely because this book was on my mind.

But that night I slept like a top and did not wake until nearly nine o'clock the next morning.

Chapter Eight

ONCE Herbert had told me of his love it was of course impossible entirely to ignore it, and since love begets love I found myself drawing closer to him, especially since we spent so many hours, unavoidably, in each other's company. He had great plans for me, and there were film notes which needed much discussion and sheer hard work.

There was in my mind no question of divorce, at least as long as the children were young. Apart from ourselves and Herbert's family there was my own family, and their feelings, to consider.

A little over ten years later we were rescued from our dilemma by Sir Alan Herbert's Private Member's Matrimonial Bill, one clause of which made desertion for three years on either side an automatic reason for divorce. By that time the children were grown-up and launched on their careers, Herbert and his wife had been leading separate lives for seven years and she herself was in any case anxious to marry someone else.

Their divorce slipped through quietly. Our marriage, at Caxton Hall, was equally quiet. Only Auntie and a very close friend, Doris Muntzer, were there to see us become man and wife. It was August 1st 1943. The newspapers had other things on their minds and in their headlines by then.

It was, perhaps, strange that I had not contemplated marriage before I met Herbert. I'm often asked in fact how actors and actresses avoid falling in love with every co-star with whom they play love-scenes. Or, alternatively, how it is possible to play love-scenes unless one is in love with one's partner!

The answer so far as I was concerned is that I *was*, with very few exceptions, and in varying degrees, in love with my film partners during those tender moments. I've already confessed to being 'madly' in love with Jack Buchanan, but that, of course, was more of a schoolgirl crush than anything. Later, as we got to know each other better, my feelings for him developed into loving friendship, and they remained that way until his tragic death from cancer in the late 1950s, when Herbert and I were neighbours of Jack and his lovely American wife Susie in Brighton. But I was aware all the time that the 'love' I felt for my fellow-stars was strictly temporary. I had only been in love deeply and sincerely once before in my life, when I was very young. In the days when I used to go dancing with Alan and his friends, among 'our crowd' was a young medical student to whom I became deeply attached. Had he been in a position to propose marriage at that time I would certainly have accepted him. But medical students, then, as now, were in no position to take on the responsibility of a wife and family, and by the time he was established enough to do so I was already wedded – to the theatre. I realise now that it wouldn't have worked anyway. I could never have lived a purely domestic life, especially as the wife of a busy doctor.

After that I was too absorbed in establishing myself to respond with more than a fleeting attraction to the numbers of personable young men I met in the course of my career. *Affaires* were frequent topics of conversation in the dressing-room. We were young, life was exciting and gay. For a few of the girls an *affaire* meant being 'alive'. But the heartbreak suffered by some of my friends when these relationships came to an end made me realise that I wanted something different – the sort of lasting love that had existed between my parents with its sense of happy security – I wanted that kind of relationship. I was fortunate. I found it and it *has* lasted.

What happened between Herbert and me during the long waiting years was that we devoted ourselves to our work and threw all our energies and emotions into making films. It's no use us pretending it was the perfect solution, or that we didn't feel strained at times, but we were lucky at least in that we spent so much time together, doing the thing we most enjoyed.

Herbert and I would not have been married on that lovely first day of August in 1943 but for A. P. Herbert's Matrimonial Reform Bill. We will never forget how much we have to thank him for.

A great man who loved the river was Alan. His house at Hammersmith Reach was the rendezvous of friends in all walks of life. His red letter day was Boat Race day when the house was packed. On one occasion I was invited and Alan met me and took me to the top floor to get the best view of the race for a long stretch. On the way upstairs we met his wife coming down.

'Where are you taking Anna?' she asked. 'Up top,' said Alan. 'Right, but no more. The floor won't stand it.' In the corner of the top room was a TV set where the race could be watched until the crews came into sight. I found myself in a corner with Charlie Chaplin, Lord Montgomery and Sir Gerald Kelly. They were as excited as schoolboys and giving their various opinions on certain aspects of the race, of which I knew nothing. They were certainly having a day out.

When back in 1932 the tour of *Stand up and Sing* drew to a close, it was to be my last stage appearance for some time, because during the next few years I was too busy filming to take off the time for theatre appearances, except those connected with films.

With the little film experience I already had, especially in *Goodnight Vienna* I knew this medium was, at least at that time, much better for me than the stage of some vast echoing theatre. For one thing, I had never been camera-conscious.

I remember once, before British and other ballet companies reached their present excellence, hearing or reading that the reason why the Russian ballet was the best in the world was that the dancers practised and practised and practised until they became completely unconscious of the movements of their bodies and 'only the spirit danced'. I feel this is the perfect description also of the best film acting: the actor has become completely unaware of exactly what he is doing and simply allows the thought to come through. 'Acting', such as is sometimes necessary on the stage of a big theatre, is death in a film. I once saw a short clip from a film made by Mrs Patrick Campbell, the great stage star. It was embarrassingly awful. She mouthed and grimaced, her gestures were exaggerated; the whole thing was grotesque. But a very good lesson to me.

The best directors, too, are not those who tell you exactly what to do. They simply keep filming the same scene over and over until all the 'outside acting' falls away, leaving the core of the character and action of that particular scene. William Wyler is one who works this way.

Herbert Wilcox, I found, was another. He just waited until I did what he wanted and then said quietly, 'Print that'. Often I myself was not at all satisfied that I had reached the stage of perfection I was striving for and asked for 'just one more shot'. Usually he was impatient of the waste of time, money and film, but sometimes I was allowed to do it again.

I remember one particular occasion when this happened. When the last take was over he asked me, 'Now do you feel better about that one?'

'Oh yes, I think that was much better,' I replied confidently.

The next morning he took me to see the 'rushes' – the uncut, unedited film of everything shot the day before. It showed me that he was right after all. Take six – his choice – was infinitely better than Take seven – mine. I didn't argue with him after that.

In time I stopped watching the rushes altogether. I always found them distressing because even in the best shots I thought I was perfectly dreadful. In the others I was unspeakable! It wasn't until the picture was edited and properly put together that I could see it through Herbert's, and the public's eyes and felt better about it. I don't think I'm alone in this. I believe Spencer Tracy for one refused ever to watch rushes of the previous day's work.

I also found that it sent me into the day's work thinking more about yesterday's work than the scenes I was about to play.

The longer I worked in show business and the more of a name I became, the more I realised, and appreciated, my dependence on the people the audiences never see: not only people like Louie and Maud Churchill our wardrobe mistresses, the hairdressers and make-up men with whom I had very personal contact, but everyone – from Producer-Director to the Tea Boy; from the most junior technicians to the Lighting Cameramen (who could do untold damage to one's reputation with bad photography). Later, when I became busier and busier I became even more dependent on even more people – secretaries who booked appointments, house-keepers who cooked my meals, made my beds and washed the dishes, chauffeurs who must get us to important appointments on time. And for me, of course, people like Jack Buchanan and Herbert Wilcox who not only gave me the chance to act in marvellous parts, but gave me the courage and self-confidence to carry them through.

Herbert had told me that *Good Night Vienna* was his greatest financial success up to that time. It cost him only £23,000 to make and in Australia alone it made £150,000. It played for thirteen weeks at the Capital Theatre in the Haymarket, and broke records throughout the country.

Suddenly one day he told me it was time to change my image – the image of the little English girl – 'The English Rose' which some critics described me as after *Goodnight Vienna* – an image which had been building up over the last few years.

'Very soon,' Herbert warned me, 'the sweetness will turn to saccharine and the public will grow bored with you. We must show them a different Anna Neagle.'

Herbert was never one to do things by halves and I have to admit that I was startled by the new image he proposed to create for me.

The Little Damozel was about a night-club singer; what used to be called a Torch-singer. The film was based on a Moncton Hoffe play. As my film partner Herbert brought over from America James Rennie, who had played the title rôle of *The Great Gatsby* on Broadway.

My rôle certainly gave me an opportunity to 'characterise' for the first time, instead of just playing myself. The Little Damozel wasn't me at all! In one scene I had to wear what was at the time a truly startling dress. Even by today's standards it might have raised a few eyebrows. It was made from transparent black net, with just a few sequins dotted about – in strategic places. Doris Zinkeisen designed it, so of course it was beautifully done. Oddly I didn't feel in the least uncomfortable in it; but then some of the costumes for the Cochran revues hadn't been exactly Victorian and I was used to people looking at a good deal of exposed Marjorie Robertson, even if Anna Neagle had been more decorously clad.

The moment the film was released The Dress appeared in every newspaper so the new 'Anna Neagle' got plenty of coverage in *that* sense.

But Herbert had not finished yet. He arranged with Earl St John, who ran the old Plaza Cinema, to put on a stage show before the film started, featuring me and The Dress.

It was an entirely new idea and sensationally successful.

Herbert gathered together a small team: myself, Scott Atkinson (a champion ballroom dancer), eight Tiller Girls, and Al Bowley, singing with Lew Stone and his Band. We worked out a routine based on a short history of popular ballroom dancing. I did the Cake Walk with the Tiller Girls, then I did the Merry Widow Waltz with Scott Atkinson . . . and finally, wearing The Dress, I went into the song and dance from the film: *What More Can I Ask?*, music by Ray Noble, lyrics by Anona Winn.

Half-way through this the cinema screen slowly came down in front of me and there I was, still singing *What More Can I Ask?* – on celluloid! Herbert had cut the titles and gone straight into the action.

It was a stroke of absolute genius and, as I've said, a staggering success.

I played the Plaza for a week, three performances a day, and we played every one to absolute capacity. Later I travelled all over the country with it, to all the big Paramount theatres (later to become the Odeons).

By the time we got back to London the film had moved into the suburbs. At one time it was running concurrently at two cinemas: the Finsbury Park and Streatham Hill Astorias, both huge places; and I was doing six performances a day, hurrying from one theatre to the other, part-changing my costume in the car, and sometimes only just arriving in time.

When I think back I wonder how I did it, but of course success is a wonderful stimulant, and now I had behind me Herbert's driving enthusiasm and confidence in me, which were wonderfully supporting.

By the time *The Little Damozel* had finished its run there was hardly a cinema record left standing, and it apparently shocked the critics into seeing me as an actress not an English Rose! My brother Alan saw it in Johannesburg. He, too, was shocked.

'What are they doing to you?' he cabled.

I couldn't help wondering what Herbert had up his sleeve for me after this somewhat shattering experience. I could never have guessed.

It was, in some ways, a return to the sweet English Rose.

Herbert had bought from Noël Coward the film rights of *Bitter Sweet*. Having seen my ability to switch from the undemanding parts of *Goodnight Vienna* to something as uncharacteristic as *The Little Damozel* he decided I was now a strong enough actress to tackle the rôle of Sari Linden. He brought over Fernand Gravet, the Belgian actor, to play opposite me. Ivy St Helier, who had been in the original stage production, played Manon la Grevette; Esmé Percy and Hugh Williams appeared while – to my delight – Stuart, as Lieutenant Tranisch, sang the famous number *Tokay*. Dear Kay Hammond was the principal 'Lady of the Town'.

Doris Zinkeisen was again responsible for the lovely dresses and Freddie Young was our cameraman.

I was frightened by the part at first, especially the singing, but Stuart and his wife Sally (who had sung at Covent Garden) coached me hard. One of my unforgettable memories of Stuart was the last day's work with him before singing *I'll See You Again*, because one of the great things about Stuart's singing was his interpretation of the words. Stuart was never content just to sing the music, the expression of the words was just as important to him. I've heard *I'll See You Again* sung often since by singers with much better voices than mine, but in my opinion they never captured the true sentiment of the song which I think Stuart gave me.

When the film appeared Herbert was accused of 'softening' the deeply poignant ending of Coward's original play and, at least for the critics, spoiling it. Herbert had no regrets. He made the film in the way he felt sure it would please cinema audiences. That was, and is, always his aim.

He started his professional life after he left the RFC as a pilot in World War I by selling silent films to cinemas in the industrial north. He spent many weary months plodding round grey, windy streets and waiting in the draughty foyers of run-down cinemas to see the managers. He knew the sort of people who 'went to the pictures' not in the very few lush cinemas of London's West End but in the shabby places across the country which were the bread-and-butter of the film makers.

I remember once when he and I were travelling north with Michael Wilding to make personal appearances with one of the very successful London series after World War II, we passed through some drab industrial town with rows and rows of small brick houses. Herbert touched Michael's arm and pointed through the train window.

'Never forget, Michael,' he said. 'The people who live in those houses are the people we are making films for, they *need* entertainment.'

Bitter Sweet entailed a very great deal of work on my behalf, not just the actual filming but a great deal of study, a vast number of costume fittings and a lot of musical work with Stuart and Sally. We decided that, happy as we were in the Maida Vale flat, it was time I moved nearer to the studios. We found *Windyridge* in Shenley, just beyond Boreham Wood: a pretty little furnished house with a garden, only fifteen minutes' walk from the studios. I took it on a three months' lease. It was from there I left to tour with *The Little Damozel*.

When I returned I found the owner was anxious to sell. By then I had completed my first contract, and Herbert had given me a second. My financial position seemed reasonably stable, and father, as a Scot, could see no better way of spending money than by buying my own home. I hadn't enough to buy the house outright, but made a substantial down-payment and took out a mortgage for the rest.

The idea that I 'hadn't enough money to buy a little house' at this stage may surprise some people, who imagined then and imagine now (perhaps with more reason) that film actors become millionaires overnight, the moment their names appear in lights. In fact, after *Goodnight Vienna*, for my first contract (for *Flag Lieutenant*) I was paid £200, £300 for *The Little Damozel* and £400 for *Bitter Sweet* – this for un-limited working hours while the films were being shot.

I did make more on the Personal Appearance tour with *The Little Damozel* but I was still far from the millionaire bracket!

However, apart from the house I was able to acquire my first great treasure, which was to bring me unlimited pleasure for many years to come: my beautiful Bechstein boudoir grand piano.

It was after *Bitter Sweet* that offers began to come from Hollywood; but Herbert felt that I was not yet ready for such a big jump. He knew that I needed careful handling and presentation still. One offer was to play the lead in *Show Boat* – and Hollywood was 'Mecca' for a movie actress.

It was disappointing, but I hadn't long to brood over it. Herbert was having another attack of genius. He decided I should play Nell Gwyn. He had made a silent version of this with Dorothy Gish which I had seen, and I knew a little about Nell from history books. Just enough to make me gasp. *The Little Damozel* had come off, I thought, but *Nell* . . .

I expect I protested, as usual, that I 'couldn't do it', but Herbert's mind was made up. This was the film which would really put me on the map; a *real* character, and a real *acting* part, as different from Marjorie Robertson or Anna Neagle as anyone could be. It was no use arguing. The only thing was to get down to work. To read as much as possible about

Nell and her times. Because if Herbert was determined I should do it I was equally determined, now, to play it authentically. At first it was dreadfully difficult. If *The Little Damozel* wasn't quite me at least she had been a singer and dancer. Nell, it is true, was an actress, but, to use her own words, she was also a 'whore'! I felt at first inhibited. Even the costume did not help much. I felt 'dressed up' for the part. It wasn't coming from inside. Cedric Hardwicke, who played King Charles, helped all he could but day followed day and I was quite unable to feel, or seem to be, Nell. Herbert was patient, just as Jack had been in the early days of *Stand up and Sing*, but I think he got pretty near to believing that he had, perhaps, made a mistake this time.

Then, quite suddenly, something happened. I don't know what it was. Perhaps I made some unconscious comment in broad cockney (I'd been brought up in an area where I heard it spoken all around me) or perhaps somewhere deep down inside me some inhibition relaxed at last and the warm tide of Nell's humour, generosity and big-heartedness engulfed me.

At the end of the first day's successful shooting Herbert stared at me in mild astonishment. 'You weren't acting Nell today,' he said 'You *were* Nell.' When it was finished Herbert took the film to America for special showings. D. W. Griffith, the 'father of motion pictures', was among those who saw it and sent me this cable:

New York, July 11 – 1934
MISS ANNA NEAGLE – BRITISH DOMINION STUDIOS –
ELSTREE – LONDON. DEAR LADY YOUR NELL GWYN IS
BEAUTY AND MUSIC NOTHING TO ME QUITE SO
WONDERFUL AS TO SEE A NEW STAR APPEAR IN A
RATHER WORN OUT HEAVEN STOP IN OTHER WORDS
YOU ARE THE CAT'S PAJAMAS AND HOW – DAVID
WARK GRIFFITH.

Herbert was full of optimism and it seemed that his optimism was justified. He telephoned me after the first showing to say that United Artists, the Distributors, predicted at least a million dollars in the U.S.A. market alone.

Then he ran into a totally unexpected snag. Herbert was sent for by the Purity League, a sort of censorship body, who insisted that the film be either drastically revised, or banned. What revisions did they require? Herbert asked. Well, to begin with, my dress revealed too much – er – 'cleavage'. It was the first time that the word was used in this particular context. 'What is "cleavage"?' Herbert asked the Purity League. 'Well – it's a shadow between two mountains,' was the reply – as they indicated my breasts. 'But that's how God made her,' protested Herbert.

Secondly it seemed that Nell Gwyn was the *mistress* of King Charles II, but never his wife? Herbert nodded. Correct – but historically accurate he hastened to assure them. His script was largely based on Pepys's Diaries, the most famous record of the time. The Purity League was not interested in Pepys. The American young must not be exposed to such demoralising ideas. Either the King married Nell (in the film) or else – Herbert expostulated.

We couldn't tamper with historical facts in that way, it was ridiculous. All right then, if she didn't marry the King she must be shown to receive her due deserts: to have died in misery and squalor. 'But she didn't,' Herbert argued reasonably, and by now a little wearily.

Then the film could not be shown in America.

In fact, it was later shown in art cinemas, cut to ribbons and with a very curious scene tacked on to the end (*not* played by me) in which a depraved Nell was shown dying in the gutter, utterly unrecognisable.

Over this sequence came the sententious caption: 'And so she lived as she wished, and died as she must . . .'

78

It would have been funny had it not been so infuriating, and costly.

What hurt me much more, though, was the attitude of one very famous and very influential critic who accused me of playing Nell without knowing anything about her. He quoted a 'fact' about Nell to prove his point.

I knew, from my reading, that his 'fact' was quite incorrect. I knew more than he did. But one does not, if one is wise, argue with critics.

I smarted, but kept silence and on Herbert's advice ceased after that to read any notices at all until long, long after the production concerned was behind us and I could view them dispassionately – and learn something from them.

'There will be lots of nice ones, some lukewarm ones, some usefully and constructively critical and a few downright nasty ones after every film,' Herbert told me, 'but knowing you, you will only remember the nasty ones and feel discouraged. So better not look at all.'

Herbert was right. I know there are people who find 'constructive criticism' a stimulus to their work, but it's true I tended to notice only the unhelpful ones which undermined my confidence.

When I began writing this book I steeled myself to go back over the old notices and was astonished to find how good they were on the whole. The *sour* criticisms were a tiny minority.

To illustrate what I mean – some excerpts of the criticisms of *Sixty Glorious Years*.

'Thank you, Miss Neagle, for an unforgettable performance. You have reached new cinematic heights.'

C. A. Lejeune (*Observer*)

'Posterity should be grateful to Anna Neagle for her performance as Queen Victoria, which will never fade.'

Walter Webster (*Sunday Pictorial*)

'Anna Neagle as Queen Victoria is magnificent. A flawless, inspired interpretation that has no equal.

Sydney Carroll (*Sunday Times*)

'Anna Neagle joins the Immortals of the Cinema for this performance – she has brought, as though by a magic wand, a great historical character to life.'

Harris Deans (*Sunday Graphic*)

'A triumph of great acting for Anna Neagle. All the time every inch a monarch – every inch a Queen.'

Richard Hastier (*Star*)

I could not wish for greater praise – yet still prominent in my memory is the notice of James Agate. Of my performance he wrote:

'Anna Neagle plays Queen Victoria as though she were a kitchen maid!'

Herbert was right! So right.

I must have been ultra-sensitive in those early years to have been so upset by them. But it's true, too, that I was lacking in confidence and needed all the bolstering I could get. One sharp word at the wrong moment could demolish my fragile ego.

Looking through an old book about the theatre recently, I came across some slashing criticisms of Sarah Siddons which quite put mine in the shade. I hope she was made of sterner stuff than I was!

Playing Nell turned out to be a marvellously *releasing* experience once I got over the hump, and it did splendid business.

I still occasionally went back to St Albans High School to visit my old head-mistress and my old games mistress, both

Top: David Wark Griffith, pioneer and greatest of film-makers at the première of *Nell Gwyn* in New York, 1934.

A rehearsal of *As You Like It* at the open air theatre in Regent's Park. I am in the centre, between Jack Hawkins and Margaretta Scott.

Above left: As Peg Woffington in one of her favourite roles, Sir Harry Wildair.
Above right: In *The Three Maxims,* a story of a circus troupe.
Below left: Peter Pan, one of my happiest experiences, at the London Palladium.
Below right: Taken with Raa, my lovely Blue Persian.

Above left: As the young Queen Victoria.
Above right: With Bernard Tussaud who immortalised me in wax for Mme Tussaud's exhibition.
Below: Filming *Sixty Glorious Years* at Windsor Castle with F. A. Young, Anton Walbrook (Prince Albert) and Herbert.

Above left: A make-up artist's miracle – as the old Queen Victoria in *Sixty Glorious Years*.
Above right: As Nurse Edith Cavell.
Below: Herbert and myself filming *Sixty Glorious Years* at Buckingham Palace. In the background is the actual carriage used by Queen Victoria and the unique Windsor Greys.

Above: During filming of *Nurse Edith Cavell,* 1939. *(From left)* May Robson, myself, Edna May Oliver and Zasu Pitts.

Below: What a cast! Gathered in Hollywood to broadcast a message of welcome to their majesties King George VI and Queen Elizabeth upon the occasion of their visit to the President and Mrs Roosevelt at the White House. Can you recognise these British stars?

Next page: Dancing with the brilliant Ray Bolger in *Sunny,* Hollywood.

SY-AAV-142

Above left: With Ray Milland who starred with me in *Irene*.
Above right: A still from *Sunny* which won the Academy Award for the best action photo of the year, Hollywood 1940–41.
Below left: I am made a princess by Chief Lookout of the Osage Tribe at Bartkesville, Oklahoma.
Below right: With Victor Mature in his first leading film role, *No, No, Nanette*.

of whom I admired very much. Herbert suggested they might like to have a little outing with me and see *Nell* after its Leicester Square Theatre run had finished and it was playing in Studio One.

Knowing their time was limited I telephoned to ask what time the programme started. What I failed to ascertain was that it was a double-bill and that *Nell* came second. We arrived a little early – just in time to see the *last* few scenes of *Nell* from the previous round. I asked whether my companions would like to sit through its companion film and perhaps see a little of the early part of *Nell* as well.

'Yes, dear, yes, that would be very nice,' they said.

After the interval the lights went down and the programme started again: with *Kermesse Heroique*, a French version, set in the 16th century, of the old Greek comedy-drama *Lysistrata*, in which all the wives refuse to sleep with their husbands until they cease waging war. It was a beautifully made film, starring that wonderful actress Françoise Rosay, but not quite what one would have chosen for one's head-mistress!

I slid further and further down in my seat until a merciful row of heads cut off my sight of the screen. Miss Archibald and Miss Lee sat stolidly through it, one on each side of me.

At all events they loved Nell Gwyn and afterwards came to the studios for a brief visit. We were shooting *Victoria the Great* and they obviously enjoyed themselves. At least instead of a brief visit, they were still there, eating bacon and eggs with us, at two o'clock in the morning!

Nell Gwyn was still in the cutting stages when Sydney Carroll, who had started the Open Air Theatre in Regent's Park with Robert Atkins as his Producer, telephoned Herbert to say that Phyllis Neilson-Terry had had an accident and would not be able to play Rosalind in *As You Like It*, due to open in ten days' time. Would I be able to take her place?

I had never played Shakespeare. I hadn't even *read* any

Shakespeare for years; but I did remember that Rosalind is the second longest female part in his whole corpus of plays. I was not used to memorising a whole rôle of this calibre. And in ten days . . .

Herbert telephoned Sydney Carroll and explained that I thought it was a lovely idea, but that with time so short . . .

Sydney Carroll persisted. Would I just come along and read a little for him? He felt I was right for the part. I was, of course, talked into it in the end, and received a great deal of help from Jack Hawkins and Margaretta Scott, who worked with me over the next week with endless patience. One interesting thing I discovered; it is much easier to memorise a long rôle by a master like Shakespeare than it is with the inconsequential dialogue of something like *No, No, Nanette*. The rhythm, the poetry and the sheer beauty of the language of Shakespeare are an enormous help. And, of course, I was playing with some of the finest actors of the day; not only Jack Hawkins and Margaretta Scott, but Nigel Playfair, John Drinkwater, Pamela Stanley, Leslie French and Robert Helpmann. We opened on Whit Monday in glorious sunshine. The lilac was just coming out. No setting could have been more perfect. I felt shaky, but excited; until I discovered that Elisabeth Bergner, considered the finest Rosalind in living memory, was sitting in the front row! Luckily I don't think the fact quite sank in during the performance.

Just before we started Herbert came round to see me. Even he looked a little nervous. 'Are you all right, darling?' he asked anxiously. I stared at him blankly.

'I can't remember a single line.'

This isn't unusual. Nine out of ten actresses (and actors) have had this complete mental black-out just before making a first entrance. It goes the moment you step on stage. But it's nasty while it lasts!

There was one thing I never completely 'got': the Epilogue

– 'Good wine needs no bush . . .' I simply hadn't had time to absorb it. My mind, by the time I reached it, was too saturated with the rest of the play.

'Never mind,' Robert Atkins said soothingly. 'We'll have it written out in large letters on a parchment scroll. You can unroll it with a flourish and read it!'

I did, and it worked.

I played *As You Like It* for a week, and the following week I played Olivia in *Twelfth Night*, which meant that whilst we were playing *As You Like It* I was learning, and rehearsing, *Twelfth Night*.

Robert Atkins said the nicest things when both plays were over and suggested I should do more Shakespeare. I think I might have enjoyed the lighter rôles. I was not so sure about my capacity to carry the great tragic ones at that point. Perhaps later on, with more experience, I might have tried. However, for the time being I was committed to the screen, and the two styles of acting are as different as nylon and tweed.

I found when I came back after the Regent's Park episode that I had to 'pull in' very much. Working in the open air demanded much bigger acting than the stage. There were microphones by now, but still one had to play larger than life; and if the wind blew the wrong way, or the trees rustled, even the microphones were not much help.

Nell was actually released while I was playing in Regent's Park, so in London that summer I was appearing simultaneously as 'the English whore' and the Lady Olivia.

The success of *Nell*, my first real acting part, gave a tremendous boost to my morale, and Herbert was quick to follow it with another acting part: *Peg of Old Drury*. Peg Woffington, daughter of an Irish bricklayer, was a famous actress at Covent Garden in the middle of the 18th century. Her *amours* were numerous, and for a time she lived with David Garrick. She was every bit as lively a character as Nell, and I loved playing her. The brogue came as easily as Nell's cockney, perhaps a little because of my Neagle ancestry, but more because we had with us, as well as Jack Hawkins and Margaretta Scott, Arthur Sinclair, Sarah Allgood and Maire O'Neill from the famous Abbey Theatre, Dublin. Cedric Hardwicke was a brilliant David Garrick. In this film I also had the thrilling experience of working on the dances with Idzikowski, a great dancer of the Diaghiliev Ballet who acted as our choreographer; a great taskmaster but a great inspiration, too. Poor Peg had a stroke on stage – while playing Shakespeare's Rosalind – and when this moment arrived in the film script, Herbert used my own panicky cry 'I can't remember a line' from my Regent's Park performance.

It was while making *Peg* that I met Tom Hesslewood, who had worked with Irving and Ellen Terry and Beerbohm Tree before becoming an advisor in the theatre on scenic design and costume. He was worried about my Peg costumes, knowing that in the 18th century, when Peg was playing, the custom, whatever the period of the play, was to wear contemporary clothes. Being a theatre purist the idea of Peg wearing a doublet and hose as Rosalind worried him dreadfully.

Herbert and I understood his anxiety. We, too, knew the 18th century theatre custom, but we also knew our cinema-going public were not all, perhaps, quite as well-versed in the niceties of theatre history. They would expect to see Rosalind in a doublet and hose, and be confused by anything different. In the end poor Mr Hesslewood gave in. One day later he came to me to report that he had talked this problem over with his wife, who had told him briskly 'Of course Miss Neagle is right. People wouldn't understand. Don't be such an old stick-in-the-mud!'

To have this link back to Irving, through Tom, was exciting. One day he and I took a day off and went down to Kent, to see Ellen Terry's house at Smallhythe. That was a lovely experience.

Peg was received with wild critical acclaim. It was given four 'stars' in the New York *Daily News* and was a big success in Chicago where it ran for forty-two weeks. It also established me firmly enough financially for me to buy my second luxury: my first car. I chose a little Daimler – the only small model Daimlers ever made, I believe. Herbert's chauffeur taught me to drive and I continued to drive that beloved car for twenty-seven years, except for the war-period, when it was laid up.

About this time Herbert became involved in forming a new Distribution Company which finally became the Rank Organisation. I am no businesswoman, and have no intention of going into the ramifications of how, and by whom, and for what reasons films are financed and distributed. I simply made the films and left the rest (except for a very short period, later on) to Herbert. The main effect on me of the new Distribution Company was the decision to make a series of deliberately 'popular pictures', including *The Three Maxims*, a cirus story. I enjoyed making this film very much, and I insisted on doing certain trapeze scenes myself instead of using a stand-in. Nothing very dangerous of course, but it gave me an opportunity to display my still quite considerable gymnastic skill. Great fun! Though dear father was, to say the least, disturbed when he came to the studio one day, and saw 'his little girl' on a flying trapeze. And how indignant he was when he read in a National daily newspaper:

'Some skilful doubling makes it appear that Anna Neagle herself did some of the trapeze work but I can assure my readers – her feet never left the ground!'

I'm afraid my Scottish blood does not qualify me as a gambler. I have, of course, always had the odd bet on the big races in the usual way of amateurs – a name that appealed to me. My Aunt, on the other hand, was quite knowledgeable. Towards the end of her life, almost the only thing which interested her on TV was the racing, especially if Lester Piggott was riding. No big bets were made, just the keen interest in watching and the delight when she found she had chosen the winner.

Herbert is not a great gambler either but, at this time, he had a permanent private box at Epsom for the Derby meetings. His overseas friends and leading film personalities loved to see the 'Durby'.

As we were not filming Herbert asked if I would like to be a member of the party. I told him I knew nothing about racing but of course I'd love to go.

His guests all appeared to be expert so I felt slightly out of my depth. However, I stuck to the 'name that appealed' formula, and ignoring their advice I backed the winner of the first two races – outsiders. I wore a bright red coat, soon to become familiar to the attendants at the Tote, where I made my 2/– each way bets.

At lunch, our table was next to the late Aga Khan's. He was known the world over as one of the great patrons of racing. This year he had two horses entered for the Derby, one was the favourite, and another was Mahmoud.

As before, I planned to back a name I fancied, so some of Herbert's guests, thinking I had a lucky touch, decided to plunge quite heavily on my choice. Before we left the table, the waiter whispered to me, 'He' (pointing to the Aga Khan) 'thinks he's going to win with the favourite, but if I were you I'd put something on his second string Mahmoud.' I switched from my 'name', backed Mahmoud, and it won! I found myself extremely popular! I then proceeded to back the winners of the next two races. One more and I would have 'gone through' the card. By now everyone in the party followed me blindly. What was I backing for the last race! I told them, and they hurried off to make their bets.

I went to the tote window, got my 2/– each way ticket but, as I came away, I heard someone saying a name that had a Scottish ring to it. It was a 'certainty'. I turned back and changed my bet, much to the delight of the attendants. By now I'd become a joke, every time they saw the red coat appear. The 'certainty' won, and I'm afraid my friends lost. But, I had gone through the card.

In *Limelight*, another of the 'popular' pictures, we had the good fortune to meet that great character Ralph Reader, who became a life-long friend. Ralph did a wonderful job when he created the *Gang Show*, and we were fortunate to see his *Gang Show* in 1935, and many since. Ralph did valuable work in the war for which he was decorated. Now he is retiring, and he'll be missed.

I didn't enjoy these popular films as much as *Nell* or *Peg*, but as is the way of such things, historical pictures were out of fashion just then. In the cinema, as with all arts, moods are constantly changing and it needs almost superhuman foresight to know what will be wanted by the time the film is shot and put together. Luckily Herbert, for almost the entire span of his Production career, had an infallible instinct for what the public would want in six months' or a year's time.

We were now in the mid-thirties, a time of depression and anxiety, not alleviated in the least by the abdication of King Edward VIII. It was felt generally in the cinema world then that the public wanted nothing more than to be 'taken out' of themselves for an hour or two each week.

Brief though Edward VIII's reign was, it gave us one great opportunity for which Herbert had long been waiting.

Chapter Nine

APPARENTLY protocol decreed that the life of Queen Victoria could not be filmed until she was three generations distant from the reigning monarch. The death of King George V removed this embargo.

Laurence Housman's stage play *Victoria Regina* had already appeared in New York and it seems that this inspired Mrs Simpson (as she then was) to ask the future Duke of Windsor why no film had been made of this colourful subject. By a stroke of luck Herbert had once made a short film of *A Day in the Life of the Prince of Wales*, and so it was to Herbert that he now gave the go-ahead to make the film of his great-grandmother's story.

When Herbert calmly announced that I was to play the part of the great Queen Empress he received the reaction he must have known was coming.

'I couldn't *possibly*. For one thing she was an *old lady*.'

'Not always,' Herbert explained patiently. 'You think of her as old because that's how your parents, and the aunts, saw her. She was only eighteen when she came to the throne. We must have a young actress to play the young part. Make-up can take care of the later years. Of course you can do it. Go away for a bit and read about her. I think you'll be in for a few surprises.'

For once Herbert was in for a surprise too; and a great disappointment. Many other people, including his new Distribution Company, agreed with me that I was not right for the rôle of the Queen Empress; that the part needed a distinguished actress of the theatre. In the end, despite Herbert's arguments, they refused to co-operate.

Even that did not shake Herbert's faith in me. His determination to make the film his way held firm. If no-one else would back his judgment he would sever all connections with the Company and finance it himself.

Which he did. It meant he would also have to find another firm of Distributors, and other studios. Herbert's own studios at Elstree had been destroyed in a disastrous fire while we were making *The Three Maxims* and Alexander Korda offered us studio-space. It was generous of him, because he too had been anxious to make a film about Queen Victoria and Herbert had 'pipped him at the post'.

He not only allowed us the space, but arranged to do so on credit, which meant Herbert would pay nothing until the film was released and the takings began to come in. But even so halfway through the film our money gave out and I threw in my own savings, sold what jewellery I possessed and worked without salary. I was still rather unhappy and very unsure of myself when I went off to Switzerland with Auntie and a trunkful of books about Victoria and her times, leaving Herbert still wrestling with the practical and financial problems. And I began to read, and read . . . books, documents, letters, diaries.

I found the latter much more interesting and helpful than the biographies, so many of which carried the author's bias one way or the other.

I also took tuition in German. I knew the earlier Hanoverian monarchs spoke English with very thick German accents when they spoke it at all. Even Edward VII had an accent (picked up, no doubt, from his father, Prince Albert). In the event I found that Victoria herself spoke very pure English, so the German lessons were never needed.

After I returned from Switzerland I also spent some days

in the House of Commons, watching procedure, so as to get the feel of the political atmosphere about which, up to that time, I knew very little.

Oddly the elderly period, like the young one, was easier to play than the middle years. Playing the part of a middle-aged woman before you reach that stage in life can be very difficult; the changes are so subtle. It is only too easy to over-emphasise the gradual slipping away of youth. I found the period following Albert's death particulaly full of problems because not only was the Queen beginning to age, but she had suffered this traumatic and potentially ageing shock into the bargain.

As both my grandmothers had died long before I was born, I had never had more than a brief acquaintance with an elderly person. To help me master the still quite difficult movements of old age I invited an aged, but vital, connection of the family to stay with me, and watched her every movement covertly: the way she used her hands; the way she sat, especially the way she rose from her chair and took the first steps away from it. The way she turned her head, or bent to pick something up from the floor.

We had an excellent make-up man in Guy Pearce but the make-up for the old Queen was still extremely complicated. Nowadays plastics and fine rubber masks have made things very much easier.

We did a test one evening after we had finished filming for the day. Guy started by putting tiny pads of cotton-wool under my eyes to make 'bags', and there was what I can only call a 'contraption' in my mouth with chunks of rubber attached to it, to fill out my cheeks, which made talking very difficult, and eating virtually impossible. Then came the intricate 'lining' work, and finally a skin of liquid rubber to bind the whole together. I had to lie on my back until this set. The whole thing took nearly three hours to complete.

It was when I looked in the mirror and saw, not myself,

but the old Queen herself, that I began to 'get' the character. I rose from my chair, almost automatically steadying myself on the make-up table, and nodded my thanks to Guy with a positively regal air!

The trouble came later. It was midnight by this time. We still had to photograph the make-up to make sure it was right, and we all had to be back at the studios by 6.30 the next morning.

I said to Guy: 'You go home now. Just leave out what I need to remove all this and instructions on how to use it.'

When I returned to the make-up room I found a collection of bottles and jars, and some notes on how to use their contents. I followed the directions faithfully, though it was a long struggle then, when I looked in the mirror again it still wasn't me. My skin was wrinkled and wizened like a very old apple. I stared at myself in horror.

Herbert came along within a few minutes to find me in floods of tears, partly from the acetone which had got into my eyes, and partly because I was so frightened. I kept saying, 'It'll never go back. It'll never be straight again.' The next morning Guy reassured me. My skin would settle down quickly he told me, which in fact it did. But I'd had a nasty scare.

The casting of Prince Albert had been a problem. Then I saw a German film *The Student of Prague* starring Anton Walbrook – here was our Albert. But could he speak English? Herbert found he was filming in Hollywood, but not happy there. He readily accepted his offer and gave a performance of both strength and sensitivity. Wonderful.

After five weeks of gruelling, almost non-stop work came a Private Showing of *Victoria the Great* at Denham studios, to a few people whose opinion Herbert valued. This was almost more nerve-racking than the work. So much hung on the result, and not only financially: Herbert's judgment, my reputation as an actress. We knew if we had failed the wolves would be waiting.

I sat beside Herbert and watched the film with growing horror. I'd let the whole thing down. I'm very susceptible to music, so perhaps Anthony Collins's magnificent score was partly responsible. Tears of despair began to trickle down my cheeks. 'What on earth's the matter?' asked Herbert.

'I'm just terrible . . . terrible. I've ruined the whole thing.'

As unobtrusively as possible he extracted me and took me up to Korda's big office, mopped me down, and talked me into some state of reassurance.

I was very sad, and moved, when two or three years ago there was a television film about Denham which showed Korda's office, derelict and falling to pieces. I remembered that evening when the world collapsed around me, and was rebuilt by understanding friends. To me that room is inextricably tied up with that night, when I thought I'd ruined *Victoria the Great* and how, after the showing was over, the guests came streaming in, saying the kindest things about my performance, and the film as a whole. I didn't really believe them at first. The kinder they were, the more I cried! I still think I was far better in the film's sequel: *Sixty Glorious Years*.

However, when *Victoria* opened at the Leicester Square Theatre it caused a furore. On the night of the première the whole Square was blocked by people. Traffic was diverted. Lord Beaverbrook, heading for his Fleet Street office, was held up.

'What's going on?' he fumed to his chauffeur.

'A film première,' his chauffeur reported. 'They're waiting for the star to arrive.'

When Beaverbrook finally reached his office he rang for the *Daily Express* Editor. 'Traffic held up in Leicester Square for some damn-fool Hollywood star,' he roared. 'Do something about it!'

'Not a *Hollywood* star,' Arthur Christiansen answered. 'An English girl playing Queen Victoria – Anna Neagle.'

'Who's Anna Neagle?'

'She used to be a chorus girl.'

'A *chorus* girl – playing Queen Victoria?' A slow grin spread over his craggy face. 'Send Holt and give it full treatment.'

They did. The next day the leader page bore the headline: A NEW NAME HOLDS UP THE TRAFFIC.

Other headlines, in other newspapers, read: 'A QUEEN RETURNS – FOR TWO HOURS'; 'A GREAT VICTORIA'; 'ANNA NEAGLE'S TRIUMPH' and 'FINE ENOUGH TO SHOW THE WORLD!'

I was by no means ashamed of having been a chorus girl; so many fine actresses began the same way: Gladys Cooper, Evelyn Laye, Gertrude Lawrence and Jessie Matthews. I *had* been afraid, at the very beginning, that it might hold me back, but then I hadn't thought the thing through. I remember reading somewhere Constance Collier's words:

'I was a superlative chorus girl because I was under George Edwardes and that is like being under Florenz Ziegfeld or C. B. Cochran, except that Mr Cochran has no chorus girls – only Young Ladies. I often wonder why he changed the title. There are so many Young Ladies in the world and so few fine chorus girls.'

I think we chorus girls owed a great deal to the fundamental training and hard work of those early days. I wouldn't have missed my chorus training for anything in the world. It gives one a sense of ensemble work. When you are trained to work as a unit that idea filters through your future work in the theatre and you learn to act for the betterment of the play as a whole, not for personal glorification.

Victoria the Great ran for over a year in London alone. I was to receive my first personal Award for it: *The Picturegoer* Gold Medal Annual Award. Former winners had been Marie Dressler, Norma Shearer, Greta Garbo (as Queen Christina), Elizabeth Bergner (in *Escape Me Never*). The year I won it the winning actor was Spencer Tracy, for *Captains Courageous*.

A fan magazine gave Herbert an Award for the Best British Film of the year.

Most exciting of all, *Victoria the Great* was chosen to represent British films at the Paris Exposition – and at the Venice Film Festival it won the Gold Cup of All Nations. The highest award.

The trip to Venice was magical. I had never been there before – a perfect film set in itself – and to go in such circumstances added magic to magic. I had a huge suite in a beautiful hotel. I can still remember walking in and smelling, for the first time, the scent of tuberoses. A great bowl of them stood on the table in the sitting-room.

We were royally entertained. After the showing of *Victoria* there was an open-air reception at the Lido followed by a banquet under the stars. There were cocktail parties, more receptions, interviews, entertainment aboard Italian and British battleships, all against this fantastic back-cloth of the most romantic city on earth.

Doctor Giannini, head of the Bank of America's film operations, himself an Italian, but now a naturalised American, was thrilled when we had a party aboard the Italian warship, with the personnel of a British warship as guests. 'Just look, Herbert,' he said, 'whilst our politicians believe we are on the brink of war – your wonderful film throws the lie back in their teeth!' Within a very short time – the same two battleships were hammering each other without mercy!

Before the Venice Film Festival, Herbert had taken the film to New York to discuss distribution plans in the States. A sneak preview in Harlem – to an audience who had arrived expecting to see a James Cagney film – had nearly caused a riot! As a great fan of Jimmy Cagney I would have sympathised with their frustration. That audience couldn't have cared less about some old English queen. Herbert protested to the cinema manager. 'Someone should have told the audience that Queen Victoria was the Queen of England – a great Queen.' 'Hell,' replied the manager, 'they don't even know where England is!' But as the film progressed it became a quiet audience – at the end a most enthusiastic one. As a result of this testing out of our film it was booked for the huge New York Radio City Music Hall, with its six thousand seats.

It was August. I was at Aldeburgh with our friends Grizelda Harvey and Monckton Hoffe, anxiously awaiting news from Herbert as to the reaction of the American distributors.

This was before Benjamin Britten made the ancient little town of Aldeburgh a world-famous centre of music. I doubt if the small post office had ever handled so many cables and transatlantic telephone calls. Day and night they were coming through. The postmaster never lost patience. He even seemed to share the excitement with me. Quite recently I had a letter from him reminding me of that time.

Upon Herbert's return there was the London opening and then we left for Venice and the Paris Exposition. Now word came that the Governor-General of Canada would be pleased to attend the North American continent première of the picture at Ottawa. Everything was falling into place. The Radio City booking was set for October, so would be preceded by Ottawa. From then on life became one huge whirl – thrilling but exhausting. Cabins were hastily booked in the *Aquitania*. Today we would automatically have flown. It is strange to think how recent a development this 'automatic' flying is. Before World War II there were, of course, no commercial civilian flights across the Atlantic. All our journeys in those days were by ship – a way of travel I still prefer – but now there never seems to be time to spare for a restful sea voyage.

As we docked in New York the press came aboard. Newsreel pictures, interviews and photographers. This was my first experience of the American press in a big way. And what a revelation. They were entirely unlike the tough pressmen I'd been expecting after seeing American films!

The distributors, RKO, had laid on everything magnificently. We left by train for Ottawa – seeing the Canadian maple trees in all their autumn glory was a breathtaking sight. At Ottawa we were the guests of the Governor-General and Lady Tweedsmuir. Wherever we went we were fêted and greeted by enormous crowds. We were escorted to the opening by a squad of Royal Canadian Mounted Police. I had the signal honour of being made an Honorary Colonel of the Black Watch of Canada. We appeared at Toronto and at Montreal, where the theatre, Her Majesty's, built in the last century, made a perfect setting for our film.

From Canada we returned to the States and the Mounted Police gave way to motorcycle police escorts with sirens blaring, ignoring red lights. I remember feeling so very small on the huge stage of the Radio City Music Hall. The Managing Director, Mr van Schmus, friend and confidant of the Rockefeller family who built and control the music hall, presented me to the audience. A vast sea of faces stretched before me. Jack Buchanan, Leslie Howard and Noël Coward among them. A night to remember.

The next morning Herbert took me over to the Music Hall. Still starry eyed after my marvellous experience, I wanted to feel again the atmosphere of that wonderful theatre. Outside, a group of young people were studying a poster. Full of confidence, we moved near them to get their reaction, just in time to hear one boy say, 'Gee, not for my money'!

In New York I saw dear 'Cocky' again – delighted by my

success he smiled, saying 'You were right, Marjorie'. There were friends of Herbert to meet – and he had many. His legal adviser, William Fitelson. 'Bill' is possibly the biggest lawyer of our profession in the United States: respected by all, feared by many, loved by a few. We are among the few. There were the Kriendlers and the Berns, who own the famous '21' Club and who always give us such a warm welcome. The wonderful Patterson family of the *Daily News*, Mary and her sisters, Loretta and Lulu. We were entertained royally by all. There were plays to see – artistes I had only read about and now could see perform. Katherine Cornell – Helen Hayes – the Lunts.

There had been tremendous changes in the city since I was there with *Wake Up and Dream*. Rockefeller Center and the Empire State Building had arisen. The Elevated Subway had gone from Sixth Avenue – sold to the Japs for scrap. Although the noise had been nerve-shattering I missed it. 'Don't worry, lady', said a taxi driver, 'it'll all come back as bombs when we go to war with Japan!'

I had a certain amount of work to do. Broadcasting – photographic sessions – newspaper and magazine interviews. Fortunately I had 'Churchie' to take care of clothes, see to packing and generally help me through. I needed her, for we were to make an extensive personal appearance tour. It was now that I began to see a great deal of the U.S.A. Before, to me, it had had only been New York. On this trip we saw something of the West, and got some idea of the courage and vision of the pioneer groups who had set out into the 'wild blue yonder' in the early days, with only hope as their guide. I talked to groups, large and small, often wondering what I could say about Queen Victoria to people living so far away, in such a different world. And I was constantly surprised, especially by the women who asked me questions about the research I had done. Had I used Baron Stockmar's diaries? Had I used the Sitwell book? Which of her journals had proved most helpful? Luckily I had read, and used, all of them and was able to say how useful in particular Stockmar's diaries had been for the character of Albert, and how interesting and enlightening I'd found Princess Alice's letters.

I had my first glimpse of Hollywood on this visit, too. The film was shown at 'The Four Star' cinema and the audience was spangled with stars.

All in all it was a wonderful experience but utterly, utterly exhausting. I was a in haze and daze long before it ended. I've no idea now how many cities we visited, how many hands I shook, how often I smiled, or talked to audiences, how many interviews I gave to the press or on radio. Little peaks of experience stick up from the general level of excitement and triumph, but after the strain of making the film, and all the travelling and changes of scene the whole thing remains in my mind as a sort of kaleidoscope of colour, noise and movement.

Victoria the Great achieved great critical acclaim in the States and Herbert was satisfied. He had done what he intended, done it well, and his judgement had been vindicated. And it did wonderfully well in the British provinces as well as London. I remember the manager of one northern circuit reporting solemnly that we had 'brought back the carriage trade to the cinema'.

Bizarre as it may sound my next rôle after *Victoria* was as Peter Pan! I went straight into this on our return from America, and I adored every moment of it. One thing particularly pleased and amused me: I had only to step out from the London Palladium, where I was playing Peter, to see across the road at the Polytechnic Cinema, the posters of my almost-unrecognisable face as old Queen Victoria!

At that time it was traditional for the first performance of Peter Pan to be given before the Lord Mayor of London, in full regalia, and two thousand of London's poor children. On entering the theatre each child was given a paper bag containing an apple, an orange and some sweets. I remember so clearly the first few moments of that opening performance. The lights dimmed, soft, atmospheric music filled the stage and auditorium. As the Darling children settled down to sleep, and I flew in through their window, the smell of oranges hit me like a blow! It was a gorgeous moment!

Throughout the scenes of action the children sat like statues, their glittering eyes fixed on the stage. They loved the flying sequences most of all, but it was obvious that the 'talking bits' bored them. The moment we went into dialogue we couldn't hear each other, or even ourselves, for the rustle of paper bags.

Peter was a joyful experience. Apart from anything else it had a sense of tradition and continuity. Sir James Barrie had only died shortly before I played the part and all connected with the production were steeped in the aura of his mysticism. If Mr Cook, the pianist, had had his way nothing would *ever* have been changed. He had seen every production from the very first in 1904 when Nina Boucicault played the part; and for Mr Cook this was the way Peter should always be played. From time to time I was congratulated, or taken to task, for doing, or not doing, things the way Miss Boucicault did them. Miss Boucicault had lent me the dagger she used when she created the rôle. In her note she had said, 'This is the little dagger which fought the pirates at the first performance of *Peter*. I would love to give it to you, but I'm far too sentimental!'

But of course we all played *Peter* differently, bringing something of ourselves to the part. I have seen a great many Peters since I played him and every actress has had her own characterisation. I saw Jean Forbes-Robertson and Margaret Lockwood play the part, and then Margaret's daughter Julia. Of all the Peters I have seen I thought Julia caught the spirit of this unique character most completely. She not only had, the longlegged appearance of a real boy, but that spine-tingling other-worldliness which for me at least gives this strange personality a haunting, disturbing, quality.

I have only one sad memory of Peter. Knowing my love of cats Herbert had given me a beautiful Blue Persian, Raa of Culloden; a great delight to me. During the run of Peter, Raa became very ill. That afternoon when Tinkerbell lay dying and I had to plead with the audience 'not to let poor Tink die' but to clap their hands if they believed in fairies, I found myself running frantically up and down the stage, tears pouring down my cheeks – as if the audience could keep alive – not Tinkerbell, but my beloved Raa.

Later in the play came Peter's line: 'To die will be an awfully big adventure,' and again my thoughts were with the beautiful creature who had left me that morning.

To be near the theatre I'd rented a small house at Hampstead. It was becoming increasingly difficult to get resident help, but a Good Samaritan friend, Dorothy Chadbourne, took over as companion-cook, assisted by a splendid daily maid – Lizzie.

Lizzie remained with us for years, always, even through the difficult war years, coping! Now in her ninetieth year her memory is still bright as ever and she has been able to remind me of many things I'd forgotten whilst writing this book.

Chapter Ten

I LOVE cats. Not that I dislike dogs – I don't. But the only dog I ever owned – a beautiful Red Setter named Mike, given me by Herbert – took me into the same police station near Elstree three times. The charge – 'sheep worrying' – the last time during the lambing season. I was warned by the police sergeant that I should keep him under control, which I'd found I couldn't as it was quite impossible to take Mike for a stroll and on a lead he almost wrenched my arm from its socket. Mike was meant to roam the fields and sheep were among his natural habitat. His beautiful soft eyes and dejected looking tail when brought to heel made me realise I'd have to part with him. We were fortunate in finding the lodge keeper at Pinewood Studios delighted to have him and he was able to lead the life for which nature had intended him.

So far as cats are concerned I'd apparently taken to them almost from infancy. I'd brought six strays into the house within a short space of time and they were presumably fed and went their way. I don't remember.

On my eighth birthday I was given my first pet cat – a short haired Blue. The family had put the kitten on a blue cushion in its basket, to greet me when I awoke. 'Widdy', for so I named her, was with us for eleven years. At that time 'speying' was apparently regarded as cruel, if not dangerous, so fifty-six kittens arrived at regular intervals over the years and finding homes for them became a major problem. She took the removal from Forest Gate to Holland Park in her stride, but the last litter of kittens was too much for her strength and, sadly, we parted with her.

I have already told you about beautiful Raa. The photograph you see on another page was published in a film 'fan' magazine. Within a few days I received a letter from a reader saying he had two kittens. Diana Wynyard had accepted one and would I like to have the other? Before I could reply, he was on the doorstep, with a small multi-coloured kitten – all cat lovers will see the significance! 'Little Puss' I named her, but in no time at all became a rather large puss and soon three kittens lay in her basket. Two homes I found but the third remained. As seems to be the law of nature, when 'Little Black Puss' – a slight misnomer being, like her mother, multi-coloured – came of age she and mum quarrelled violently. Both went into 'an interesting condition' at the same time. I put their baskets at opposite ends of the warm garage – even screened them from each other. Coming down early one morning, there were two purring mums sharing one basket and contentedly feeding thirteen kittens! We never did know which belonged to which. Aristocratic Raa was in no way involved, having been 'taken care of'. But he loved them all – as though he had been responsible for the lot. Even taking his turn with the washing.

Herbert was already planning to follow *Victoria the Great* with another film about the great Queen. There was still so much material untouched he felt confident that we could do this without repetition, and that the crowds would come flocking in even greater numbers after the success of the first picture.

Meanwhile in February 1938 with my aunt and an old friend Doris Muntzer I went to Madeira for a short break.

Father had finally decided to take a trip to Australia and New Zealand – something he had wanted to do ever since his enforced retirement. He planned to visit old friends from his sea-faring days and also meet Alan and his wife in South Africa. When a few years before he'd remarried we were all delighted knowing that, although he never complained, he must, at times, have been very lonely. So now he and Dorrie, his wife, were on their way back, due to stop off at Maderia for a few days with us.

I found Madeira wonderfully relaxing and the stay there helpful in a way I'd never have imagined. One evening after dinner a woman with an air of elegance and distinction paused at our table and asked whether we would take coffee with her and her daughters in the hotel lounge. She proved to be Lady Elphinstone, elder sister of Queen Elizabeth, then Queen, now Queen Mother. She told me that she had recognised me, and that she had seen *Victoria the Great* at a private showing at Windsor with the rest of the royal family. In some trepidation I asked whether we had made, despite our strenuous efforts, any bad mistakes since we were denied facilities. She shook her head, smiling. Only one very small thing. The servants in the Palace would not bow or curtsey to passing royalty. They would simply ignore them. I heaved an audible sigh of relief!

Father did not, in the end, join us in Madeira. During the voyage home he had suffered a second heart-attack and was too ill to land. So instead our little party joined his ship and we travelled home together. As my step-mother was ill at this time too, it was decided that she would go to Bournemouth to recuperate and Stuart arranged for father to go into a nursing home at Hampstead for treatment. Stuart and Sally lived at Hampstead and I had rented a small house there the previous year. So it was to Holly Mount that father came from the nursing home and we both had the joy of seeing a great deal of him during the last year of his life.

Herbert had arranged for the screenplay of *Sixty Glorious Years* to be written jointly by Miles Malleson and Sir Robert Vansittart, adviser in chief to the Foreign Office.

Apart from being a very fine writer the latter was strongly

opposed to the policy of appeasement then being pursued by Chamberlain and was glad to lend his support to a project which would, he felt, help to remind us all of our heritage.

Herbert explained to Sir Robert how necessary it was to have facilities which had not been available to him on *Victoria the Great*. Vansittart saw the King, telling him of the proposed film. The result was that Herbert was advised he should write personally to the King, setting out his requirements, which he did.

The King replied, granting the requests and finished his letter by saying: 'If you propose showing the scene of Queen Victoria leaving Buckingham Palace for the drive to St Paul's Cathedral on the occasion of her Diamond Jubilee *would you mind* using the Windsor Greys – any other horses would lack authenticity.' And so, as the old Queen, I rode in the actual carriage used by Queen Victoria, behind the unique team of Windsor Greys. Herbert has read this letter when we have appeared with the film in many parts of the world and it never fails to make a profound impression of the courtesy and understanding of King George VI. It was arranged that Sir George Crighton, a gentleman-in-waiting, be with us throughout the production and the King asked the Dowager Countess of Antrim to help and advise me on all matters of Court etiquette.

With Lady Antrim, a lady-in-waiting to the Queen during the last ten years of her life, I went to Windsor Castle. She was full of fascinating anecdotes about this strong-minded and sometimes unpredictable lady. She delighted in 're-staging' some of her experiences for me and describing in great detail Victoria's clothes and mannerisms. Princess Helena Victoria, a grand-daughter of the Queen, talked to me too, and showed me many precious mementos of grandmother. We studied portraits of her, hair-styles as well as clothes and general appearance, and altogether went into far more detail than we had for *Victoria the Great*, for now we had greater facilities and felt we could come even closer to the truth. Today, with the exception of Princess Alice, Countess of Athlone, I doubt if there is anyone living who was close to the Queen, or old enough to remember personal details.

I had already visited Balmoral once before. In 1933, after *Bitter Sweet*, father suggested that I should take a restful trip to Scotland, by coastal steamer. At the time I had of course no idea that one day I should return to play Queen Victoria. It was *just* a holiday.

The voyage was every bit as restful as father had forecast and I shall never forget one particular evening when we crossed the border at Berwick. The glow from the sinking sun turned the scene into a blaze of gold and brown beneath a sky of darkest, clearest blue, making me feel we had moved not just into the ambit of another country, but another world.

It was four years before I began my study of Queen Victoria and when I came to the reading of her Highland Journals it was with a feeling of sympathetic understanding that I read the Queen's description of her own first trip to Scotland in the *Royal George*.

From Aberdeen I had motored to Braemar and spent ten unforgettable days at the Invercauld Arms, where I learned something of the character of the local people; the innate dignity and sensitive receptivity of the Highlander. During that stay I watched the Highland Games, and later suggested that as Queen Victoria had once commanded that the Games be held at Balmoral we should incorporate the colourful sequence in the film. This Herbert did. When the time came two to three hundred local people were needed to recreate a realistic picture and one of my friends from that earlier visit to Braemar, Colin Gordon, the village cobbler, proved himself a tower of strength in persuading and cajoling the reserved people of Royal Deeside to take part in the 'play-acting'. To our delight they brought out from old family trunks, clothes which had been stored, some of them, for a century: a plaid, or kilt, a jacket or bonnet, belonging to a grandparent, or even earlier forbear.

With the years the tartans and velvets, dyed from natural dyes, had softened into the most beautiful and subtle tones. We were, when the film was shown, to receive letters from Scots people all over the world, telling us how deeply moved they had felt when watching this all-too-brief sequence.

Mrs Gregor, owner of the Invercauld Arms, was wonderfully kind to me during my first visit and I spent several evenings listening to her reminiscences. From her early girlhood she had visited the Castle and she had many stories to tell of the Queen's visits to Balmoral; happy days of shooting parties and picnics.

We stayed with her during the filming. One evening, returning from the Castle in the twilight still wearing my make-up, I met Mrs Gregor in the entrance hall. For a moment I thought she was ill. She stood, transfixed, white-faced, staring. Suddenly she whispered 'The Queen – she has arisen.' Very reassuring for a young actress almost overwhelmed by the responsibility of the rôle she was playing.

Our first visit to Balmoral itself began rather inauspiciously. We had, naturally, obtained permission first and the housekeeper, Miss Gilbert, had been warned of our coming. When we arrived Major Ross, the Factor, telephoned to say we were on our way. Sir George Crighton accompanied us. At the front door there was a huge iron bellpull, which we tugged. Presumably it tolled sepulchrally somewhere in the depths of the building though we heard nothing from outside. We waited uneasily on the doorstep: Sir George Crighton, Herbert, myself, Anton Walbrook, Freddie Young and our Art Director. In due course the door opened, just an inch or two, and we caught a glimpse of a little, rather severe-looking lady, neatly dressed in grey.

'Yes, what is it?' The tone was not exactly welcoming.

Sir George explained our business. Miss Gilbert looked round the group.

'D'ye *all* have to come in?'

'Well – yes . . .'

'Then wipe yourrr boots; ye'll dirrty the cairrrpets,' Miss Gilbert instructed, opening the door a little wider.

Sheepishly we 'wiped our boots' and crossed the threshold. As Balmoral was closed for the season, inside all was darkness, each window shadowed by a thick blind. We peered about in the gloom until Sir George suggested mildly that we might have a little more light.

Reluctantly Miss Gilbert crossed to a window and pulled up a blind, stating somewhat defensively ' 'Tis the page's worrrk to raise the blinds, not mine. But he's away on holiday at the moment.' We felt he might almost have been summoned back from Foreign Parts to carry out his duties!

Between us Sir George and I made one dreadful error. As we were walking along a corridor a little painting caught my eye. 'Who's that?' I asked. 'Is it Prince Charles Edward?'

'I don't think so,' Sir George answered, peering closer. 'I think it must be the Old Pretender.'

Miss Gilbert drew herself up to her five-foot-nothing and in a voice of thunder demolished him completely. 'Please dinna use the worrrd "Prrretenderrr" beforre *me*!'

Gradually, however, she softened towards us and later, when we were filming, was kindness itself. On the last day, when I was rapidly reaching the end of my tether, the sun refused to shine for a very important exterior shot. I had a splitting headache from the noise of hundreds of people milling about and the anxiety of watching the clouds for a break sufficiently long for a reel to be danced or a caber tossed.

Miss Gilbert noticed my distress. 'The puir wee bairrrn,' she whispered to Herbert. 'Let her come to my room for a cup of tea and a little peace.' As we went towards the Castle, she ran ahead, clapping her hands and calling imperiously for 'A cup of tea for Miss Neagle . . . a cup of tea for Miss Neagle.'

In her room I rested, drank my tea, and recovered. Until I was myself again I doubt if she would have permitted even Herbert to call me out to do a scene – sun or no sun!

When filming at Balmoral was completed and we finally drove away, we turned to wave to Miss Gilbert, a tiny grey figure standing in the now wide-open doorway of the Castle. To me she will always be the embodiment of all the loveliest qualities of the Highlander: not too quick to make friends, but having once accepted us, indefatigable in doing all she could to make us happy and comfortable.

Before going to Royal Deeside we had already completed scenes at Windsor Castle, Buckingham Palace and Osborne, receiving everywhere every possible co-operation, down to the detail of permission to fly the Royal Standard over whichever building we 'occupied'.

There was one delightful moment during the shooting of a scene in the Courtyard of Buckingham Palace when two excited young faces appeared at an upstairs window, watching the proceedings with enormous interest. I often wonder whether the Queen (as she is now) and Princess Margaret recall that morning as vividly as I do!

Sixty Glorious Years was made entirely in Technicolour, which added a great deal to the vividness of the film. *Victoria the Great* was in black-and-white, except for the final reel, when colour was used to stress the joyousness of the Jubilee. The sudden switch then was electrifying and again, I believe, added greatly to the film's impact.

After the two Victoria films I was touched by the number,

not only of letters I received, but gifts large and small of Victoriana. Some of them were very precious: a pair of silk stockings with drawn threads and the embroidered monogram 'V.R.'; a small tooled leather note-book shaped as a cross, with the then Princess Victoria's own handwriting (this a gift from the son of the Queen's Maid-of-Honour, Lady Reid). The Princess had written in it herself: 'Dear Mamma gave me this on the 20th May 1824.' Then there was a miniature with the young Queen's head on one side and the old Queen's on the other; a tiny Almanack and note-book carried in the Queen's reticule in 1897, a gift from Lady Antrim. When I was invited by Bernard Tussaud to be modelled for the famous Exhibition I was thrilled. During the blitz Tussaud's was hit, and my nose melted in the fire! When repaired I remained on view for some years as the Young Queen. Later, I was given the waxen hands from the model, which I keep still on a velvet cushion. The effect would be eerie, were it not for the delicacy of the modelling.

Queen Mary attended the opening of *Sixty Glorious Years* in October 1938, with the Duke of Kent and Lady Antrim in the royal party. Lady Antrim wrote me a charming letter afterwards to say how pleased they all were. Queen Mary was then the Queen Mother, and thirty-five years later, in 1973, another Queen Mother, the present one, was to see a special Gala Performance of the film with crowds almost as big as those attending the original première. Autumn 1938 was not the happiest moment to release a film depicting the glories of the Empire's past. Munich was upon us, and though a year's breathing space was snatched from Chamberlain's visit to Germany, there was an uneasiness in the atmosphere.

The critics, however, were kind. 'This is not only the best film ever to come out of a British Studio, it is the best film to come out of any studio in the world' was particularly generous praise from *The New York Times*. Of my own performance the London *Evening News* wrote: 'Anna Neagle triumphs in a film which makes history – and makes history live.'

There were so many more in the same vein that it is now heart-warming to read them, but a little embarrassing to quote them! But most of all I prize Lady Antrim's letter, part of which I quote:

Dear Miss Neagle,

I find it difficult to tell you how greatly I admired the film last night. It is a wonderful presentment and your part was beyond word, excellent. You carried out youthful enjoyment and want of experience and some self assertion with a dignity which grew with the years. The gradual responsibility of mature years and increase of power with old age were splendidly carried out – while your presentation of the dying Queen was a marvellous exhibition of realisation. The expression on a face when life is passing was so real – the task accomplished – the heavy burden laid down – the fatigue which made it welcome – I saw it all with tears in my eyes – it struck me as artistically perfect. I am not a critic and speak as one of the crowd, but this is how it affected me and I can only thank you for taking me back to ten years of my life when I was with a beloved mistress. I have written to Mr Wilcox to thank him for giving me a very great treat. Yours very sincerely,

Louisa Antrim.

Chapter Eleven

AFTER we had taken the film to America, and returned, I made a series of personal appearances. It was during this tour that word came to me that father's condition had worsened. Strangely I had awakened during the previous night, feeling sure he was calling to me – though I'd be the last to claim psychic powers.

I was making an appearance at Glasgow and fortunately decided to take the night train home. He rallied a little and talked to me quite happily about his boyhood and early days – and was able to listen to an interview I was doing on a BBC programme with Gracie Fields. As Stuart was also broadcasting that night, he heard for the last time Stuart singing John Masefield's words:

> I must go down to the seas again
> to the lonely sea and the sky –
> and all I ask is a tall ship
> and a star to steer her by.

It was the end of an era for us in many, many ways.

I will always be grateful that I saw so much of my father during the last few months of his life. Sometime earlier he had had to give up his work as a marine surveyor, which involved climbing down holds of ships to get to the cargo, and as he so hated being idle, Herbert suggested he take over my business affairs, including tax and banking operations. At the time the income tax from my services was quite big and I never had any pretensions to a business head, so I jumped at the idea, knowing how meticulous father was, and so completely honest. Father made a great success of his new job, although he was bewildered by the size of the income. When I said he was completely honest there were moments when he was too much so. One day he asked me to sign a cheque for the Inland Revenue and with it was an Income Tax demand dated only the day before! 'Don't you think you should check up on this and see if it's all right to pay?' I asked him. 'Of course not,' he replied. 'These people are not fools. They know what they are doing. They don't make mistakes.'

I signed the cheque.

A few weeks later a rebate for a substantial sum arrived from the Inland Revenue – they had omitted to make agreed deductions for my various professional expenses!

On another occasion my accountant, and our very dear friend Vallance Lodge arranged a conference with an eminent tax counsel, Heyworth Talbot, to explore whether I should take up residence outside the United Kingdom, or form a Company outside. The chambers with the book-lined walls, the comfortable leather chairs and the talk of section this and that of the Income Tax Act had a soporific effect on me. My father was listening attentively. I'm afraid I dozed off. I came to after my momentary lapse to hear him saying quietly, but very firmly, 'My daughter does not wish to live outside this country and while she is here she will pay her tax like everyone else.' They tried to explain, but father was firm. 'My daughter has no wish to evade her tax,' he told them. 'But we are discussing avoidance – not evasion,' put in Heyworth Talbot. But father would not budge and had his way and I have never regretted that he did.

One day when a new contract was signed I decided we would have a day out. A sentimental journey to Arundel where father ran away from home as a boy and became a seaman. He hadn't been to Arundel for forty or more odd

Top: Herbert and me back in England with Amy Johnson's parents filming *They Flew Alone*, 1941.

Centre: Recording the thrill of meeting Amy Johnson shortly after her historic flight to Australia.

Bottom left: As Amy Johnson in *They Flew Alone*.

Bottom right: See overleaf!

Far left: Just married! Herbert and myself, 1943.
Top: At an American Air Base in England, 1944, with the crew of the *Lady Anna* which I christened with a bottle of beer!
A scene from *I Live in Grosvenor Square* with Rex Harrison.

Top: Robert Donat's presentation of Jane Austen's *Emma*, St James's Theatre, 1945.
Centre, left to right: One of Doris Zinkeisen's imaginative costume designs for *Nell Gwyn*.
The white evening gown, designed by Gladys Calthrop, in *Emma*. The beginning of my
film partnership with Michael Wilding in *Piccadilly Incident*, 1946.
Bottom: All time record crowds for *Spring in Park Lane* at the Old Empire, Leicester Square,
1947.

Dancing with Michael Wilding in the fantastically successful *Spring in Park Lane*.

Top: Michael, Herbert and myself – triple National Film Award for *Spring in Park Lane*.
Centre left: When Laurence Olivier and I had each won the Picturegoer Gold Medal Award for the fourth time.
Bottom left: Spencer Tracy presents me with the Gold Medal Award for *The Courtneys of Curzon Street*. We had shared this honour in 1938.
Centre right: The Gold Cup of All Nations awarded at the Venice Film Festival for the Queen Victoria film, 1938.
Bottom right: Posing with Auntie 'Bill' Neagle on the day of my C.B.E. investiture, 1952.

Top: With thirteen of the awards won by myself and Herbert including my first Gold Medal Award for Queen Victoria.

Left: With Norman Hartnell and wearing the lovely wedding gown he designed for *Maytime in Mayfair.*

Upper right: As Betty in *Elizabeth of Ladymead,* a role which shocked filmgoers.

Lower right: Sitting for Jacob Epstein *(Photograph by Ida Kar).*

Top: With Odette at a deserted village near Annecy where so many had been shot by the Nazis as a reprisal *(Copyright Waugh Illustrated).*
Herbert, Peter Ustinov, myself, Odette and Trevor Howard filming *Odette.*

years and found it practically unchanged. He literally glowed with nostalgic pleasure. 'I must see if Claude's shop is still here,' he said. Claude's father had been the local butcher. The shop was still there – and we walked in. Sawdust on the floor – the old-fashioned wooden chopping block and the butcher, back to us – striped apron, white coat and the customary straw hat. 'Hello, Claude,' said father.

Claude turned round, joint still in hand. He had not seen father since they were boys. 'Hello, Bert,' he said as though they had last met yesterday, and got on with the job. 'Changed the shop a bit, haven't you Claude?' said father. 'Oh, you mean the old shop. This is the new one. Been like this forty years now.'

When father had come to stay with me at Hampstead the little house was just a stone's throw from the Round Pond – the delight of boys with model boats. I can still see father who had carried troops from New Zealand and Australia to the Dardanelles and who commanded the first refrigerated meat ship plying between Uruguay and England, showing an enthusiastic young budding mariner how to get the full benefit of wind in the sails.

Another unforgettable moment was when I saw father and my uncle, Arthur Neagle, sitting on the front at Kingsgate – binoculars glued to their eyes, watching an English vessel rounding the North Foreland. A running commentary duet of sea lingo passed between them of which I understood only a very few words. The occasion was a happy one in 1936 when I took a furnished house for a brief holiday, with Auntie 'Bill' coping with the household matters, father and Uncle Arthur, who you may recall, introduced him to my mother, his wife Aunt Tommie who served under Nurse Cavell as a nurse in the London Hospital and who died only recently, aged 103, two cats, Rona our maid and myself. The last occasion on which the Robertsons and the Neagles got together.

Chapter Twelve

OUR American Distributors, RKO, were so pleased with *Sixty Glorious Years* that they felt it was high time I went to Hollywood, to be introduced to the American people in a big way. Even after such important pictures as *Nell* and the *Victorias* I was still known only to a minority of the vast American public. Publicity was an industry of its own there and I would, without question, benefit from their expertise in that field.

Herbert was convinced that the time was ripe, though he was adamant that I should not be taken over by the American film industry.

He agreed that it would be beneficial for me to play with well-known American personalities, so after lengthy discussions and negotiations, it was decided that we were to form the first Anglo-American co-production company, in Hollywood, and we all worked together amicably, and very successfully.

Herbert went ahead of me to explore the ground and have preliminary talks about possible subjects. In March, 1939, I received a cable to say that he had decided to make a new film about Nurse Edith Cavell. He had already made a silent version based on Reginald Berkeley's *Dawn*, with Sybil Thorndike. This was a subject which greatly appealed to me and I went to the Imperial War Museum and began to research with a sense of happy anticipation. The Curator, interested in the project, suggested I should get in touch with Miss E. B. Wilkins, O.B.E., who had been Nurse Cavell's

Assistant Matron in Brussels from 1912 until they were both arrested in 1915. Sister Wilkins, after extensive interrogation, was released. Back in England, by 1939, she had become Matron of a small cottage hospital at Chard in Somerset. My correspondence with her and later my visits to her were fascinating, and most useful. I set off for Hollywood feeling that I had done my homework well. When I arrived I found that, so efficient were the Research Department of the Hollywood Studios that they were ready with sketches by Eddie Stevenson of the actual clothes worn, photographs of hair style for Mel Burns, the make-up chief, and drawings of locations, the original Depage Clinic at Brussels. In fact, a marvellous job of research had been carried out.

Two of the smaller parts in the film were filled in a most interesting way. On an earlier trip to America, staying with Joseph Schenck, head of Twentieth Century Fox, we found that his butler, a Belgian, had been butler to Brand Whitlock, the American Minister in Brussels at the time of Nurse Cavell's arrest and execution. He well remembered two of the nurses (one had been Miss Wilkins) arriving at the American Embassy in great distress on the night of October 11th 1915, to beg for help in saving the life of their Matron. He played 'himself' in the film.

Another small character part was played by a man who had been in the same prison, at the same time, as Nurse Cavell. He remembered how, when she was taken out for execution the other prisoners banged on their cell doors in protest, knowing, through that mysterious grapevine which grows in prisons, what was about to happen.

We also had in the cast a German sergeant who had *been* a German sergeant in the 1914–18 war. Hollywood was so cosmopolitan that it could produce at least one example of the real thing whoever, or whatever, it was!

Portraying the character of Edith Cavell made an indelible

impression on me. I have always had a great admiration for nurses in general, but Edith Cavell and Florence Nightingale, whom I was to portray later, were I think to influence my own character in a way no other people, certainly no other film characters, have done, apart from another war heroine about whom I shall write later: Odette.

Nurse Cavell always had with her a copy of St Thomas à Kempis's *Imitation of Christ*, in which she marked certain passages of key importance to her. When she died she left her copy to her favourite cousin. When Sybil Thorndike played the rôle, Cousin Eddie showed her Nurse Cavell's original volume so that Sybil could copy the markings into her own: Sybil passed them on to me. My copy of the book still lies on my bedside table and has proved a great inspiration, especially in times of trouble.

One thing did distress both Herbert and myself. With war on the horizon we intended this to be an *anti-war* film; when it was shown, our intentions were frequently misunderstood. We were often either accused of, or congratulated on, making war propaganda – the *last* thing we had in mind.

When I went to France in 1945 I was told that *Edith Cavell* was showing in Paris when the invading troops arrived and that Herbert and I were immediately put on Hitler's blacklist.

More comforting was the letter I received in 1946 from Mlle Bihet, Superintendent of the Edith Cavell–Marie Depage Institute for nurses in Brussels, to say that she had received permission to project the film each year on October 12th, as an example to successive generations of nurses. This institute had been in the planning stage when Nurse Cavell died, and the 'Marie Depage' who shares it as a memorial was her friend, and wife of the doctor with whom she worked. Marie Depage was drowned when the *Lusitania* sank off southern Ireland. She had been to America to collect funds for the Belgian Red Cross.

I enjoyed working in Hollywood. Everyone was very professional about their work, and enthralled by the idea of making something so realistic.

But it was not just the professionalism, it was the kindness which made me happy. A number of odd-job men worked around the studios, one of their jobs being to blow a whistle for the doors to close for silence when a scene was about to be shot. They were a varied crew, one from Northern Ireland, another from England, others a mixture of races.

Each morning when I went into my little dressing-room on the studio floor, I found a tiny posy of fresh flowers on the dressing table. A charming thought. Then, one morning when I turned up a little early, I discovered their origin. One of the odd-job men had just arrived and was still holding the posy awkwardly in his large hand. It seems they had been taking it in turns to bring flowers from their own gardens.

'Oh, that *is* kind of you,' I said.

'We just wanted to make you feel at home,' he said, putting down the flowers and sidling from the room.

I got the impression that everyone, right down to these men, was totally involved in the picture; it was *theirs*, and it mattered terribly that it should turn out well.

Twenty-six years later, in October 1965, I was asked to give an address from the pulpit of Norwich Cathedral on the 50th Anniversary of Nurse Cavell's death. After World War I her body had been brought home and buried in a very simple grave in the shadow of the Cathedral walls. It was one of the most moving, most responsible tasks I have ever undertaken and an occasion which will stay with me. I had visited Miss Wilkins a few months before her death in February 1965, and so still felt close to the happenings of 1915. I refreshed my memory by re-reading Miss Cavell's poignant letters to her nurses from prison, and the marked passages in the *Imitation of Christ*. Then Herbert and I spent ten days in Norfolk, soaking in the atmosphere of the countryside, mercifully little changed, in which she grew up. We visited her birthplace, and the little church where her father preached, and met a very elderly postman who still remembered her.

The beautiful old Cathedral was packed to capacity with war veterans, nurses in their scarlet cloaks, the Chairman and Committee of the Edith Cavell Homes of Rest for Nurses, the widow of the padre who had given Nurse Cavell her last communion, old colleagues, family and friends.

Together we sang her favourite hymn, *Abide with Me*, and remembered the woman whose life began so unobtrusively as daughter of a Vicar of a tiny Norfolk hamlet, and ended in a blaze of shocked publicity before a firing squad, for doing what she conceived as her simple duty as a nurse: saving lives.

The occasion was, I suppose, the more emotional for me because of its setting. Cathedrals have always deeply affected me, partly I believe because more than most children I attended so many during my impressionable growing years. At St Albans I regularly attended services, and it was here I was confirmed. It was here, too, that I first heard Stuart sing the words of Christ in Bach's *St Matthew Passion*. If I shut my eyes and sit alone quietly I can still conjure up that scene, and that wonderful voice. It was music which somehow opened up a new realm, making intangible things seem tangible.

I was to hear him sing it again about a year before our mother died; the week before Easter. Again in a Cathedral, this time St Paul's. Deeply ingrained in me too is the sadness and pride of attending his Memorial service at St Paul's, early in 1959.

I think it is the music, combined with the sheer size and grandeur of Cathedrals; the way the chords roll upwards magnificently into the roofs, and echo back again, which touches my deepest being.

In an entirely different way I remember a *little* cathedral Herbert and I visited whilst on holiday in Jamaica; the little 18th-century wooden Cathedral of Montego Bay which has, alas, since been destroyed by fire, but where on that occasion we were stirred once more by the old Nativity story, simply played by a negro Joseph, a negro Mary, and a little negro Christ. The night before, Christmas Eve, we sat on a patio at our hotel; the sea lapping within yards of our feet. A silver path of moonlight stretched to the horizon. Away in the distance came the sound of singing.

'Si - lent night. Ho - oly night . . .'

Out of the darkness a barge cut across the ribbon of moonlight. A cross gleamed and around it the black faces of the cathedral choir upturned above their snow-white surplices. We sat very still as the music swelled up, then faded.

Yes, I think it is the music – and the sheer age of most cathedrals, as well as the realisation of the centuries of work 'to the Glory of God' which went into their building, which moves me so much.

A few days later we were awakened by a knock on our door. 'A telephone call for Mrs Wilcox from New York, Sir.' It was the Consul General.

'In confidence,' he said, 'as you are away from England, I have been asked to inform you that His Majesty the King has approved your appointment as a Commander of the British Empire in recognition of your services to British films. Congratulations.'

My name was in the New Year's Honours list in 1952, exactly a year after Herbert had received his C.B.E. And therefore we became the first husband and wife to be so honoured.

Chapter Thirteen

THIS was the first time I actually worked in Hollywood, then, the Movie Capital of the world. I found a number of surprises in store for me – mostly pleasant – though I still doubt the wisdom of meeting one's screen idols in the flesh. It can be very disillusioning! One often comes to like them enormously as people, and still admire them as actors, but something of the illusion goes. In fact, when I had an opportunity of meeting who was, to me, the greatest of them all – Greta Garbo – I hesitated, she was somehow too magical. What I did instead, when my aunt and I went on holiday in Scandinavia, was to visit the shop where she worked before beginning her acting career. Alas, I found no plaque on the counter commemorating her presence!

There is, of course, a distinct possibility that Miss Garbo would not have wanted to meet *me*. The 'wanting to be alone' legend was no publicity stunt. She lived a withdrawn life. Even during the shooting of a film she could not bear to have any but the most essential technicians and actors around her. What is more, she could sense the infiltration of some outsider on to the stage, however discreet, and was unable to continue working until he or she had left. May Robson had acted with her in *Anna Karenina* and told me how Garbo had gripped her hand when she had sensed someone not actually a part of the unit, was in the Studio. Dear May Robson hadn't been aware of this, but sure enough there was someone at the far end of the stage she'd not seen before.

One idol who did not disappoint in real life, although that

is too strong an expression to use, was Gary Cooper: even better-looking off-screen than on. Those eyes! I suggested that he might come to England to make a film one day. His answer: 'Aw, you're always stopping for tea over there. Wouldn't suit me!' It is true that in Hollywood everyone seemed to work even harder than we did in the English studios, and heaven knows, we worked hard enough.

I never quite recovered from being a film-fan myself, and to be surrounded by such giants as Jimmy Cagney, Spencer Tracy, Paul Muni, Hedy Lamarr, Bette Davis, Joan Crawford, Carole Lombard (so soon to die tragically in an air crash), Ginger Rogers and Fred Astaire was a constant excitement and stimulus.

On one visit I had the utmost delight in meeting the legendary Gish sisters: Lilian, the serious one, and Dorothy, quite the wittiest woman I've ever known, as swift with repartee as writer Dorothy Parker.

One of the stories about Dorothy Gish's wit I particularly like for its subtlety is told of her visit to a very new, very glamorous, very 'everything' house built by a current star on the summit of one of Hollywood's hills, where every glass of water had to be specially pumped up from the valley. Notwithstanding this, every bedroom had a bathroom (fitted with radio, as well as the usual offices). There were *two* heated swimming pools with constantly changing water, and even an artificial trout-stream where guests could catch their own trout for lunch. After the grand tour Dorothy flopped into an armchair and her hostess asked anxiously: 'Well, what about it?'

Dorothy looked at her solemnly. 'It's a lie,' was her only comment.

Dorothy had made pictures with Herbert in England including the silent version of *Nell Gwyn*. Herbert adored her.

Another very witty, very *pretty* girl I met when I first

started filming in Hollywood was Lucille Ball. Everyone in the studios loved her, but she never seemed to get anything much to do. RKO gave her bits and pieces but never anything to show off both her talent and her extraordinary beauty. The chief hairdresser said to me one day, 'Do you think Mr Wilcox could find something for Lucille in your picture? We're all sure she only needs a real break.' There just wasn't anything in the Edith Cavell film so we never worked together. Eventually RKO terminated her contract and she went to another company – to return some years later and with (I feel sure) a very justifiable sense of triumph to *buy out* RKO and re-christen their studios The Desilu Studios, where so many enormously popular and successful television series have been made.

I was impressed, incidentally, by the respect shown to the 'greats'; and the general formality towards them. No Christian names here, as there had been at home. Gregory Peck was always 'Mr Peck'. A few had affectionate nick-names. Clark Gable was always 'King' and Spencer Tracy 'Spence', but this was unusual. I was never 'Anna' in Hollywood except to my intimates. I was always 'Miss Neagle'. Some years later when Irene Dunne was filming *The Mudlark* in England she attended the National Film Awards (Herbert had won an Award that year) and she remarked afterwards how odd it was to hear so many people address me as 'Anna'. 'It sounds so affectionate,' she said, a little wistfully.

But I understood why the Hollywood stars stood a little aloof. With their gigantic popularity, life would have been insupportable without this slight distance. They couldn't go anywhere without being besieged by admirers. In addition to the formality I found them generally reticent in conversation; very reserved.

One of our more interesting excursions from Hollywood was to *Pickfair*, the mansion built by Douglas Fairbanks

Senior and Mary Pickford at the height of their fame. Mary Pickford was no longer the World's Sweetheart of course. She was by then one of the world's most efficient and successful business-women. Visiting *Pickfair* in the late 1930s was rather like visiting royalty.

It was while we were working in Hollywood that the war clouds grew darker and in the end it became obvious that war *was* coming. The British artistes, who included Laurence Olivier and Vivien Leigh, naturally felt anxious to return home. Herbert and I were involved in a very extensive promotional tour of the Edith Cavell film which took us to even more places I had not seen before and it was while we were in Ohio that Hitler's troops marched into Poland. We had already been warned by a Reuter correspondent that England was likely to be involved, but found it difficult to believe. We had left home in April, long before there were any real signs of war preparations. The Munich Agreement, we believed in our innocence, had put an end to any such possibility.

When war was actually declared on Sunday, September 3rd we were appalled. The whole thing seemed so unreal from that distance.

After the opening of the film at Washington, Lord Lothian, then British Ambassador, sent for Herbert to congratulate him on Edith Cavell as a 'first-rate propaganda film' and asked our plans. 'To return to England at once,' Herbert replied promptly. Lord Lothian demurred. 'I think it would be better if you carried on here for a while. It is more than possible that film-production will cease in England for a time as it did in the '14–'18 war, and I think you could be of more use here, doing what you do well, than returning to England as "untrained labour".' Herbert, of course, had flown with the Royal Flying Corps in World War I but aircraft had changed a good deal since then, and Herbert himself was a little older. My own instinct was to volunteer for the W.R.N.S, but the

Directive from Washington included me too, so it was back to Hollywood, at least for a time.

Stuart had been invited to do a broadcast on an American net-work the previous month and had stayed on to visit us in Hollywood. Incidentally, he was the first singer to make an experimental transatlantic broadcast in the mid-1920s. Naturally Stuart wanted to get back to Sally and the children, but he was included in the Directive.

For Herbert and me the question was what sort of films should we make? *Not* propaganda. Perhaps something light, bright and escapist, to cheer up the troops and munitions workers. In all, we made three of these gay, frothy films which did exactly what we had planned for them: *Irene*; *No, No, Nanette* and *Sunny*.

Herbert had a second reason for making light, charming, song-and-dance films, a little more selfish perhaps than the first. So far American audiences had seen me only in character parts and believed me to be a middle-aged character actress. These new films were to blow that 'middle-aged' image sky-high and present me as myself, which the heads of RKO felt would really put me over in a big way in the Hollywood style.

Incidentally, I was reminded of the American reaction later, during a continental ENSA tour, when a young soldier was heard to remark: 'Cor – last time I saw her she was Queen Victoria. I never knew she had legs like that!'

As with *Edith Cavell* I was surrounded in the new films by American players too. In the *Cavell* picture we had George Sanders in a powerful rôle, Edna May Oliver, Zasu Pitts in one of her few serious parts and May Robson. Of all the women I met in Hollywood, I believe dear May Robson, 'Muzzie' May to all, who had played Apple Annie in *Lady for a Day*, one of Frank Capra's greatest successes, was the dearest and most amusing.

She was seventy-seven years old and in her previous film

with John Barrymore he had to dump her into a swimming pool and sit on her until she was submerged. Jack thought it great fun – so did 'Muzzie' May. But after a number of takes the doctor said she had had enough. At seventy-seven more than enough I should say. After our film she was offered a seven-year contract by Jack Warner. 'Seven years,' said 'Muzzie' May. 'What if I'm not here?' She wasn't. She died shortly afterwards but denied strongly her illness had anything to do with her swimming pool episode with Jack Barrymore. Although by the calender she was seventy-seven, 'Muzzie' May was all of twenty in real life; never missed a party and always giving them. I talked to her about the obsession the press seemed to have for revealing the age of artistes, but it was not only the press, she said, telling me in her own inimitable way of a personal appearance she was making a year before. As she came out of the stage door a crowd was waiting for autographs. She noticed a very very old lady, really very old, waiting. 'Muzzie' May was quite concerned and went over to her. 'I am sorry to have kept you waiting. They should have brought you in to see me.' 'That's all right – my dear' – the old lady muttered. 'I just wanted to touch you' (which she did). 'You see, my mother took me to see you when I was a little girl!'

Edna May Oliver was a tremendous personality, slightly eccentric. She had her own caravan on the stage and a maid to prepare all her food in bags. Nothing must be contaminated by contact with water or pans. 'You're eating poison, my dear,' she would say in her own inimitable manner, as I enjoyed my studio snack.

Ray Milland co-starred with me in *Irene*. Like Lucille Ball he was having difficulty in getting off the ground. He was under contract to a rival studio but they were content to let us have him – although with a warning: 'We shan't be taking up the option.'

He was absolutely right for our film, and made a huge succes in it. When it was over Herbert told him the story of how we managed to get him.

'Right,' Ray said. 'I've never been allowed to drive my car through the front gates of the studio. Next time the doorman tries to stop me, I'm going right on in.' He did. What's more, he parked outside the Chairman's office! When Herbert tried to get him for our next production he wasn't available, he was co-starring with Claudette Colbert! I last saw Ray during the run of *Charlie Girl*. 'Don't let her know who's here,' he told the Stage door keeper. 'Just say "A friend would like to see her."' What a glorious surprise – I adore Ray!

I did another long personal appearance tour with *Irene*, singing and dancing *Alice Blue Gown*, which I also sang on the radio with Bing Crosby – what a thrill that was! This *Irene* tour was a combination of promotion for the film and Appeals for War Relief. America was already sending Bundles for Britain and Red Cross Aid.

I performed at the Lockheed aircraft factory where a fund was started by the workmen which called upon everyone there to donate a dime from their wage packets every pay day. A huge factory employing thousands. Soon there was enough subscribed to pay for an aircraft which was sent as a gift to Great Britain.

I was asked if I would go to San Francisco to attend a race meeting. The organisers would have the big race named 'The Anna Neagle Stakes' and the proceeds of the day would be donated to Bundles for Britain. Naturally I accepted. I was to place a laurel wreath over the winner's head.

Then came a very dramatic and emotional experience. On the West Coast of the United States there had been a legendary horse named 'Malicious'. 'Malicious' was a strange creature who seemed to be disinterested in racing. He would go up to the starting point, under pressure, and was reluctant to join in or take part in the race. When the starting signal was given, 'Malicious' seemed to say 'What are all those fool horses doing? I'd better go along and see', and he would join the race way behind all the others. Coming into the straight, 'Malicious' would prick up his ears and, despite being a long way behind, he would overtake one by one, and a shout would go up from the crowd, 'here comes "Malicious".' And he would be first past the post.

I can't vouch for it, but legend has it that 'Malicious', the lazy horse, disinterested in racing, was never beaten. He retired to an easy life on the farm, ten years or so before this story.

When the horses for the Anna Neagle Stakes were announced, there were six runners – one was 'Malicious'! A moan went up from the crowd.

To bring 'Malicious', the unbeaten, out of retirement, without a chance of winning was unfair. But they had overlooked the affection for their idol. One by one the number of runners was reduced as every owner scratched his entry, leaving the field open to the old horse.

'Malicious' came out looking rather like an *old* shire horse, his hooves hardly visible under his long hair. The starter's flag went up and everything happened as before. 'Malicious' ambled off lazily. And then, into the straight. The cry went up from the crowd as of old, 'Here comes "Malicious".' Up went the ears and he shot forward passing the winning post in grand style, as in his days of glory.

When I put the laurel wreath over his head they told me there wasn't a dry eye.

Even the bookmakers shed a tear.

At our Hollywood hotel, El Royale, one entire suite was set aside and donated to the Bundles for Britain Committee – at a time when hotel accommodation was in very short supply. The generosity of Americans in giving of their time, as well as money, was very heart-warming and it showed how they felt for us 'Limeys' in war-time. The above are three typical instances.

All these appearances helped us to know Americans well, we like to think. In all, we visited forty-seven states. But we were anxious to get home and do what we felt was a real war job. Laurence Olivier had started flying instruction. Richard Green crossed the Canadian border to join the Army. Stuart was to do this the following year – which is why he served in the Canadian Navy.

Irene was an enormous success and proved to be, as we hoped, just what everyone wanted. To this day it is *Irene* so many Americans remember me by. As recently as this year, on several occasions Americans, seeing *No, No, Nanette* at Drury Lane asked to have a word with me to tell me how much they had enjoyed it all those years before. With *No, No, Nanette* and *Sunny*, in which I danced with Ray Bolger, we felt we did a useful job of cheering people up. I collected a few small personal tributes that year too. I was voted Best Dressed Actress of the year for the lovely clothes designed for *Irene* by Eddie Stevenson; was the first actress to appear on the cover of *Life*, and became an Indian Princess! To the Osage tribe of Oklahoma I am known as Wah-Sha-Wah-Wah Ko-Ki-Iki. I still cherish my bead head-band and feather with which the Chief invested me, together with the interesting prayer rug he placed round my – the 'Princess of the Dance' – shoulders.

After the colourful ceremony, we stayed overnight with Mr and Mrs Phillips, a prominent Bartlesville oil magnate. The next day they took us out to their ranch for lunch. When we arrived we were met by the ranch manager. Our host asked where his grandson was. 'Oh!' the manager hesitated. 'He-he had made a previous date – asked me to say he was sorry.'

Some time later, whilst we were being shown around the

ranch, the manager, having, I suppose, decided that I would accept what he proposed telling me in the spirit in which it was intended, said: 'When I told young Jim his granddad was bringing out a film star, he was all hepped up – wanted to know who was coming. I said I thought it was a British actress, Anna Neagle. "Gee" he'd answered. "I wish it was Hedy Lamarr." And, I'm afraid, he went out!' It certainly struck me as funny, if not exactly flattering.

After the war, we were back in Hollywood on a short visit. At a party we met Hedy, looking an absolute dream of beauty. I laughingly told her of the Oklahoma incident. Her reply took me completely by surprise. 'Oh,' she said, 'you embarrass me!' Not at all the reaction I'd expected!

On location at La Quinta in the desert we visited a Fair and were astonished to see a team of Shire horses. The wizened little man with them told us in a broad Devon accent that he'd come to the U.S. as a groom in 1911. How homesick we felt!

When the war had begun to hot-up in 1940, the British Colony in Hollywood became even more restive. In May Belgium fell, then Holland. In June came Dunkirk. Still we were told to 'get on with the job' until, in desperation, Herbert, Cedric Hardwicke, Cary Grant and Laurence Olivier went to Washington to ask for a new Directive. By then there was a new Ambassador, Lord Halifax. He was sympathetic, but not much more helpful. Anyone of military age, with specialised qualifications such as flying or engineering training, should return to England. He added, somewhat deflatingly, that England could not cope with 'unnecessary' people. There was for one thing too much of a food problem already. Eventually Larry took his pilot's licence and early in 1941 he and Vivien returned to England. It was mid-August before we managed to get our permits.

Chapter Fourteen

OUR Atlantic flight took twenty-nine hours, via Bermuda, the Azores and Lisbon. Our stop-over in Portugal was one of the strangest experiences I have ever had. Being officially neutral, Lisbon was a gathering place for all the nations on both sides of the conflict. We were dining one night with an English journalist when he suddenly lowered his voice.

'Just behind you, the one who looks like a schoolmistress, she's quite a prominent German spy.'

The next night we dined at a table alongside a Nazi Minister who was entertaining both Italian and Japanese Ministers.

Going up in the lift one day I became conscious that the only other occupant was very much a German officer, and tucked under my arm was a copy of *Berlin Diary*, by William Shirer, New York Foreign Correspondent in Germany up to the U.S. entry into the war. This is the copy from which excerpts were published in the *Daily Express*. It hadn't been seen in England as, of course, this was prior to the attack on Pearl Harbour and the States were still neutral.

We had some very odd encounters indeed in Lisbon. We ran into Gracie Fields (with whom I had done a short Canadian tour in 1940) to find that she – one of the highest-paid entertainers in the world – was absolutely flat broke. Luckily, after a few back-of-an-envelope calculations we found we could lend her fifty dollars? Gracie was also awaiting the flight home.

After three days in this curious no-man's land we flew on to England by KLM. That fine actor Leslie Howard was to die later on a similar flight. It is always assumed that the Luftwaffe thought Churchill was travelling in the same aircraft, and they shot it down.

When we landed at Bristol, we saw the effects of the war on England for the first time. Parts of Bristol were virtually non-existent and, apart from Coventry and Liverpool, probably bore more of the brunt of the Blitz than any provincial city. Since so much of the all important aircraft industry was located there, I suppose dear lovely Bristol was a legitimate target. However, it made us very sad.

When we arrived in London we learned that the head of RKO in England, and his whole family bar one, had been wiped out in a raid. 'Windyridge' was by this time crammed. Auntie Bill had insisted that her two sisters, a sister-in-law and my cousins must come there out of the midst of the Blitz that was then at its height in London. The girls had, of course, to go to their jobs in town, but 'Windyridge' was undoubtedly safer at night.

It was a small house but we made room for me until I started work on the picture Herbert was planning – the story of Amy Johnson.

There was much to hear of the families' experiences. All we had been reading in the States had never quite conveyed some aspects of the situation – the sheer day-to-day difficulties. The horrors of the Blitz and the humour and courage with which it was being faced by the ordinary men, women and children we had – at a distance – understood. Now we marvelled anew.

Alan, who had been recalled to the Royal Navy from South Africa at the outbreak of war, had been on a short leave whilst the cruiser he served in was somewhere in Britain, so there was news of him. But most of the time he spent in other waters. Shortly before we got back he had been involved in the disastrous evacuation from Crete. Of course, I hadn't known this, although at the time it happened I had 'sensed' something. Again, I must emphatically disclaim any psychic gifts! Alan was now in hospital at Alexandria, making a rapid recovery and, apparently, the life and soul of the place. I learned this later from a nurse I met who looked after him. She told me there was 'never a dull moment'. I could well believe it! Dear, humorous, happy-natured Alan.

As our next film was to be made at Denham Studios, we found a furnished house at Gerrard's Cross and soon Auntie and I, together with Lizzie and her husband, moved in – transport being such a problem in war-time, it eased that difficulty.

Back in England we were, of course, encountering for the first time the deprivations of rationing, and I appreciated all the more a gesture made on my leaving America, when the RKO President had presented me with a box clearly labelled 'orchids'. How charming, I thought at the time. When I opened the box it proved to be more thoughtful and understanding than charming. It was full of lemons – absolutely unobtainable in the U.K.

Feeling that we should get to work as quickly as possible we wrote to Amy Johnson's parents. They could not have been kinder, or more helpful, though it must have been a painful experience for them as Amy had been killed only a few months earlier that year whilst ferrying an aircraft from the Blackpool airfield to an R.A.F. station near Oxford. We met them in Hull, where Amy had grown up, and they took us to see their old home and Amy's school; talked to us about her background and introduced us to hosts of people who had known their daughter and could talk about her from personal knowledge, and different points of view. Among the people we met were Lord Brabazon, and Amy's old employer William (later Sir William) Charles Crockett, Pauline Gower, Head of the Womens' section of the A.T.A.

The Johnsons were by then no longer living at Hull and our next meeting was at Blackpool, where they then were, to be near their third daughter, Mollie, wife of the local Town Clerk. This was, incidentally, the place where Amy spent the last night of her life.

Amy's mother had always kept a room for her in their Blackpool home and it was here I was put to sleep, surrounded by her 'things'. They had a tiny projector, masses of film of Amy, as well as still photographs, letters and souvenirs of her adventures, all of which called up a vivid picture of the girl I was to portray. Later they lent me her flying suit and an opal ring she wore 'for luck' on every flight but her last.

Rifling through the photographs I came across one with Amy and myself side-by-side, taken just ten years earlier, soon after her record-breaking flight to Australia and my own breakthrough in the theatre and cinema. We had both been invited to attend the opening of the speedboat season at 'The Welsh Harp', Hendon. Amy was blunt about it. She was not interested in personal appearances. She wanted a serious job in aviation. 'But,' she confided in me unhappily, 'they don't want me to fly. They only want me to do this sort of thing.' Her disillusionment was understandable. One only had to throw one's mind back to 1930 to remember the anxiety as the world awaited news of her. Remember, aircraft were not equipped with radio – difficult for younger generations to realise, I imagine. And the unparalleled welcome when she arrived back at Croydon. Only her father and a mechanic saw her off. Hundreds of thousands lined the route on her return.

We had also to get permission to impersonate her husband, James Mollison, still flying with the A.T.A. (and doing other secret work for the Air Ministry which I think has not been sufficiently acknowledged). When the film, called *They Flew*

Alone, was finished Jim was invited to a private showing. Herbert asked his opinion. 'I thought you caught Amy's spirit exactly,' he said to me. 'And your own?' Herbert asked. Jim paused. 'Well,' he said, 'he lifts it a bit, doesn't he?' He made a graphic gesture with his elbow.

'Well – didn't *you*?'

Jim grinned. 'Well, yes I suppose I did!' And, of course, he did, though it never seemed to impair his brilliance as a pilot.

Robert Newton played the part in the film. It was, alas, a bit of unsuspected type-casting. Bob, too, 'lifted it a bit'.

I can still remember his first arrival at the studios, straight from a mine-sweeping voyage; still wearing his uniform as an able-bodied seaman. I innocently believed at the time that his nautical roll was the result of a recent voyage on rough seas. I little realised how many rough seas lay ahead of us together! But he gave an extraordinary performance. He was a most original actor and all his characterisations made a great impact on audiences.

Bob was given three weeks' leave to make the film. This was quite common practice during the war. Actors and actresses who joined the forces were frequently given short periods of home-leave to make films: it was the only way to keep the industry going and turn out entertainment for both troops and civilians who came increasingly under fire and strain.

There was a special showing for Amy's parents. We had promised not to release it without their approval. I did not attend the showing. I waited, back at Claridges, where we were to meet for a discussion. Herbert told me later that, when the lights went up, no-one spoke.

I was waiting, on tenterhooks, desperately anxious to know the Johnsons' verdict. They arrived at the hotel. A kind kiss from Mrs Johnson – but I could see she was under emotional strain.

Mr Johnson then said: 'May I speak privately with my wife?'

By now we were both feeling quite sure that they disapproved of the entire film.

We waited for what seemed an age before they came back. Amy's mother's eyes were pink-rimmed. I looked at her dumbly, miserably. I had tried so hard to do Amy justice . . . Suddenly she put her trembling arms round me and I heard Mr Johnson say to Herbert: 'Thank you for giving Amy back to us again.'

Poor Amy! In spite of her great achievements, and they were prodigious, she never felt that her abilities were used to the full until perhaps those last few months of her life when, as a member of the Air Transport Auxiliary, she had ferried aircraft to the R.A.F. She was only thirty-seven when she died, but I think in many ways this was the death she would have chosen. At least she was at last doing something useful, and doing it for England. She was always extremely patriotic.

Her father told us a poignant story of Amy's last night at Croydon, before she took off for the epic flight to Australia. She kissed him good-night and asked him to knock on her door at 4 a.m. next morning.

On his way to do so he realised that Amy had never been out of England in her life – and now she intended to fly to Australia!

At 4 a.m. he was outside her door. He knew that if he did not knock she would not take off for several days, as the predicted winds were unfavourable. In that time he might yet persuade her not to go. If he knocked her up and she took off – it would be practically sending her to her death. He hesitated for minutes and then knocked.

He also told me the sad story that when Amy came down in the Thames estuary in the fog and the rescue boat was almost near enough to touch her hand, she had called out to the man in the boat 'Hurry up", but had been swept under the ship, never to be seen again.

One of the things I did in 1941 was for Howard Thomas of the BBC. He masterminded a very popular programme – *The Brains Trust*, apart from creating the idea of a girl singer having a common link with the fighting forces – Vera Lynn. Howard presented her as the 'Sweetheart of the Forces'.

He had heard of my being a guest on an American Radio programme called *Information Please* in which, under the chairmanship of Clifton Fadiman, were Oscar Levant, P. G. Adams and a college professor. It was one of the most popular programmes in the States – so much so that several short films were made of it and it was launched in great style at Radio City Music Hall. It was a unique compliment to be invited to appear on *Information Please* and I was suitably flattered and, of course, accepted. Apparently I did well.

The panel of the BBC *Brains Trust* under Derek McCulloch was Jan Masaryk of Czechoslovakia, Julian Huxley, Hannen Swaffer and Professor Joad. A formidable team. I could not but accept such an invitation.

A completely political question was put by the chairman. Right up the street of Jan Masaryk, but having just returned from Canada and made aware of this very problem, I went ahead and to the astonishment of the panel answered the question at length. Masaryk laughed and said to the Chairman 'Please ask me something about British films and I hope that I can answer it as well as Miss Neagle did that one.' Howard Thomas, who did such a fine job for the BBC, did not know that my experience on *Information Please* was not exactly the success with me that it was with him. In flying to New York to record and film the programme, I hadn't sufficient time to get my hair done so I decided to wear a hat – a very distinctive one with a huge white flower.

The session went so well, that the producer made extra episodes and everyone was delighted. Except me. At San Diego where Herbert and I saw the third episode a woman in a high-pitched voice said, 'She has the same hat on!' – and of course, I had – but it took a woman to notice it! About this time I had the pleasure of meeting, and working with, Bebe Daniels and Ben Lyon, whose war-time *Hi-Gang!* did so much to keep up Britain's spirits. Herbert and I took part in two of their radio programmes. I remember going round to their house in Bayswater for a conference with their Producer and Script-writer, though so far as I could see it was Bebe who did most of the writing! I can see her now, tucked up in the corner of an enormous sofa, sparking off ideas.

After the conference we had a meal, then Bebe took me up to her bedroom. 'How are you for make-up?' she asked. (This was a perennial problem, like so many other shortages.) 'Not too bad,' I said, 'though flying from America meant I couldn't bring much. I'm getting a bit short of mascara.'

Bebe climbed on to a chair and reached down a box from a high shelf. 'Here you are. I've got some. Take this.'

No-one who has not lived through the war years, with their quite incredible shortages, right down to boxes of matches, can appreciate that gesture. To me it epitomised Bebe's warmth and generosity. She had, after all, only met me for the first time that day.

Our recording of that programme in a BBC studio in Lower Regent Street was interrupted by an Alert. We were all ushered out to sit on the stairs, the safest place in the building! Then one of us looked up. No roof! We shot back into the studio. At least that had a ceiling!

Herbert had promised Air Marshal Bishop, his C.O. in the R.F.C., to return to Canada to do a tour for his Air Cadet Corps and now set about the tedious business of obtaining permits and some way of re-crossing the Atlantic.

At last all was arranged, but we were warned that the utmost secrecy about our movements must be kept, for everyone's safety. Unfortunately, when we made our second *Hi-Gang!* broadcast the fact that we were due to leave for Canada slipped out.

The result was that the start of our journey was accompanied by what now seem quite ludicrous precautions. We were to sail from Gourock for Halifax, Nova Scotia. When our train arrived in Glasgow, I was whipped into the station-master's office and from there whipped to an hotel where I was not allowed out of my room. My meals were sent up. Next day the same thing happened. Back to the stationmaster's office, swiftly into the train and lastly, slightly breathless, and feeling I should be wearing a false beard, aboard the *Batory*, a Polish ship with an all-Polish crew apart from Captain Symons, the British Liaison Captain. The Polish Captain, Deyczakowsky, we did not meet until we arrived in Canada. He spent the entire voyage on the Bridge, or cat-napping in the Chart Room; but we did learn that he had snatched his ship out of Gdynya from under the very noses of the Nazis on the day they entered Poland. Since then he had been involved in the Norwegian landings and evacuations, amongst other jobs.

Captain Symons very kindly made available his cabin for the Canadian Trade Commissioner's wife and me, so we were more comfortable than I'd expected to be. The ship was carrying some three thousand R.A.F. en route to Canada for training under the Commonwealth Training Plan which had been pioneered by Air Marshal Bishop. Billy was almost alone in being an airman of the 1914–18 war not regarded as an old fuddy-duddy and was accepted by the young generation of airmen.

We were a tiny convoy, just the *Batory*, one other ship, the *Letitia*, and two escorting destroyers. The *Letitia* was carrying German prisoners of war and Canadian wounded. Our 'cargo' consisted of the R.A.F. recruits.

Strangely enough, I felt alarm only once on this voyage. There was certainly no sense of sustained fear; more a sense of adventure. But one night, when I was singing *Alice Blue Gown* during an impromptu concert, there was a terrific explosion, as if the ship were being ripped apart. There was no panic at all. A Flight Sergeant with a fog-horn voice shouted 'Quiet!' Everybody laughed and we simply carried on. Perhaps we were by this time 'bomb-happy' or merely resigned. We discovered later that there had been signs of a submarine in the vicinity and the two destroyers had closed in on us, and dropped depth charges. When we were discussing the crossing with Captain Deyczakowsky at Halifax, he told us we had been more in danger of being rammed by our own escort than torpedoed by the enemy!

The crossing had lasted eleven days. From Halifax we flew to Montreal to meet Air Marshal Bishop, also Stuart and Herbert's son John, who had been busy with preliminary arrangements.

The show was called *Celebrity Parade* and was a mixed programme of music, dance, a Noël Coward play – *Still Life* (*Brief Encounter*) and finally another short, very patriotic play: *The Lady who wishes to be known as Madam*, by Monckton Hoffe, introducing characters from British history. Amongst them, of course, I played Queen Victoria, Helena Pickard played Florence Nightingale, Herbert Marshall was the Narrator and Dennis King the Duke of Wellington. Colin Keith Johnston played Nelson and Bob Coote the 'Tommy' soldier. There was plenty of humour in the play and it ended on a high note of patriotic drama, with a back-cloth of St Paul's Cathedral lit by the fires of the Blitz, and on-stage groups from all the Services.

Air Marshal 'Billy' Bishop was a tremendous personality. V.C., D.S.O. and 2 bars, M.C. etc., a whole row of ribbons, credited with bringing down seventy-three German planes, which did not affect his sense of humour or his efficiency in getting things done.

One-night stands of *Celebrity Parade* were envisaged from Toronto to Victoria. Billy was a great war-time pilot but he was also a great beggar. He persuaded the Canadian Pacific Railway to donate a complete train free of all charges. He laid on the R.C.A.F. Band of eighty-four, and all food and hotel accommodation was donated. He came with us and talked to the audiences and the objective was to raise $50,000. On the first night at Toronto we raised $97,500 – at Montreal $65,000, and by the time we reached Victoria the gross amount had reached $245,000. Much of this was due to Billy's own efforts. His air cadets' uniforms and training facilities were safe and Billy was most grateful. They were his pilots of the future – his 'young eagles'.

Apart from all else he was a good psychologist. No discriminate entertaining for Herbert and me to meet the VIPs and ministers to help our cause. His house at Ottawa, presided over by his lovely wife, Margaret, had a patio with a perpetual glowing charcoal barbecue – steaks of all sizes were on the table – some salad and rolls. You picked your steak and cooked it yourself, whoever you were – gin and tonic to drink or soft ones. Mackenzie King, the Prime Minister, often patronised the barbecue. When I was cooking my steak a woman next to me said 'I enjoyed your Queen Victoria film very much.' I turned. It was Princess (now Queen) Juliana of Holland. 'Thank you, Ma'am,' I answered. 'Which one did you see?' 'I saw them both,' she said. 'The colour made *Sixty Glorious Years* a bigger spectacle, but I liked the simple love story of *Victoria the Great* so much.' And she went on about certain comparisons of both films that really amazed me. She asked me, 'Is it true Kaiser Wilhelm saw the film at Doorn? We understood he did.' 'Yes, Ma'am, that is true.' 'Did he express an opinion?' she asked. I told her that he 'expressed his great astonishment and appreciation at the true to nature representations of his grandparents, the Queen Victoria and the Prince Consort.' 'You must have been very pleased,' said Princess Juliana. 'We were, indeed,' I replied. Princess Juliana smiled and finished up by saying, 'My mother is a great admirer of Queen Victoria and in many respects of the same character.'

I didn't tell her that the letter, signed by a representative, had been sent 'By Command of the All-Highest'. The former Emperor of Germany had been exiled, living in her country, by courtesy of the Princess's mother, Queen Wilhelmina, since 1918.

It would take a whole book to tell of that wonderful tour of Canada. The Rockies, the flat wheat belt of Manitoba, the beauty of Lake Louise, our visit to the headquarters of the Royal Canadian Mounted Police at Regina, the charm of Victoria. And, everywhere the welcome extended to us. We had friends at Victoria so stayed on a few days, then returned to Toronto to make arrangements for the journey to England. This was a problem. Air Marshal Bishop was at his home on Lake Muskoka and it was quite a distance. Herbert telephoned him and at once a flight was arranged. All so easy, we thought; of course he'd arrange it overnight. The plane proved to be an open cockpit, two-seater. The bush pilot flying her appeared, like Amy Johnson before him, to have only a school-type map. I was in the minute seat behind him. Herbert beside him. To me it seemed a miracle that we landed right at Billy Bishop's house by the lake. The permit wasn't quite so easy to obtain, even through Billy. So, Herbert had to travel to Washington. I went back to Toronto to await developments. But at Toronto I found there had been a cable awaiting me for some days from Alan. When the tour had started at Toronto I'd written him telling him of plans and the interesting trip out and that I'd be home again by the end of the year. His cable was peremptory, 'Stay where you are, you don't know what you are doing!' He was probably right. But we were lucky.

At last our permission to go home came through. We had to wait for three days in Halifax, ready to leave at the proverbial drop of a hat, and we wandered around in the fog; an experience which was to be most useful when we came to make a film called *The Yellow Canary*.

There was the usual secrecy and security surrounding our departure and the call finally came at ten o'clock at night. It was November and pitch-dark, and it was not until we were aboard that we realised that our vessel was a banana boat of five thousand tons, *The Cavina*, with a sea-dog of a captain, Sam Brown. Our fellow passengers, were all R.A.F. personnel. I had the minutest cabin I'd ever seen, until I saw Herbert's – which was even smaller. We asked with sinking hearts, how long the voyage would take. 'Oh, anything up to three weeks,' we were cheerfully told.

The next morning, when light came, we found ourselves off New York with an enormous convoy. We counted fifty-six ships, with two destroyers on either side, almost out of sight.

Two days out from New York we went on deck and looked round. No convoy! In some alarm we asked what had happened. 'Oh,' we were told airily, by one of the crew – 'we couldn't wait for that lot. We've just gone ahead . . . '

Forty-eight hours later we finally managed to catch up with 'that lot'. It was a bad crossing, and claustrophobic as we were rarely able to go out on deck because of black-out precautions and rough seas. One wave actually caved in part of the ship's side, carried away some of the rails and a precious life-boat, and triggered off the alarm system.

Off Ireland the convoy broke up. Some ships went to Glasgow, some to Liverpool. We were Cardiff-bound. As we drew near to making land-fall a plane flew low overhead. Apparently our naval escort had confirmed that Herbert and I were on board and we were asked to go to the Bridge so that the air crew could send us a signal. As we waved, the plane dipped its wings, and our naval escort drew in alongside so that the crew could wave 'Goodbye'.

The frigate that escorted us into home waters also sent a message. Smoke was pouring from her stack and it was quite evident she had no reserve of speed. The captain sent a signal 'Don't tell anyone but we're flat out, so don't go so fast!'

When we arrived back we went right into production on *The Yellow Canary*. Casting this Herbert felt there was a small but excellent cameo part for Margaret Rutherford. We knew she had left *Blithe Spirit*, in which she had made such a sensational success, because she needed rest and we were delighted when she accepted. 'Just one day's work,' Herbert had assured her agent. But, so happy was she with Herbert, and he with her, that he wove Margaret's character into an integral part of the story which ran right through the film! So there was little rest for her but she was gayer and fitter at the end than when she started the picture. What a loss the theatre and films suffered by her death. Such a unique talent and lovable person.

My part was a great change for me. The daughter of parents prominent in the War Office and WVS, I appeared to be spying for the Nazis. It was not until the last few moments of the film that it became clear I was, in fact, doing secret intelligence work for the WRNS. Richard Green was released from the Army to play in it with me. I was so busy that I did not see the finished film for nearly a year. Then I caught up with a matinée performance in Newcastle.

Sitting in front of me were two ladies, one very elderly and rather deaf, so that her companion was constantly explaining what the film was about, to the accompaniment of low moans from her elderly friend. 'Oh no. Tch-tch,' she muttered. 'Oh dear me *no*, Anna Neagle would never do that.'

When I finally appeared in my WRNS uniform, and all was made clear, she gave a very relieved sigh. 'There,' she said, turning in triumph to her patient neighbour, 'I *told* you Anna Neagle wouldn't do things like that.'

On this tour I had an opportunity of seeing something of my Robertson relatives at Glasgow.

Shortly before the war Herbert and I had been invited to visit a big exhibition at Hampden Park. It was winter so I felt a dark suit, fur coat and hat would be suitable attire.

Now, in 1944, again I was invited to attend an exhibition at Hampden Park – an Army exhibition. What to wear? It was a blazing hot August day so I wore the only thin dress I had with me. To complete the outfit there was a hat with a large rose and high heeled shoes. As I teetered around the rough paths, having tanks and guns explained to me by the C.O., I felt a complete idiot. Amongst the crowds I spotted my cousins. I waved self-consciously. I was to have tea at my aunt's house before going on to the theatre and when I arrived I was greeted ecstatically by my younger cousin who, with her charming Scottish burr cried 'Oh! Cousin Marjorie, you look a real film star. When you came before it was so disappointing – you looked just like an ordinary person.'

Two lessons taken and absorbed!

Chapter Fifteen

FOLLOWING *Yellow Canary* I was due to do an ENSA tour of Britain. Before setting out we just managed to squeeze in our quiet wedding, a brief honeymoon in Falmouth, and our move to the small Victorian farmhouse Herbert had owned for many years but which had been let to tenants for the last seven years.

Basil Dean, the head of ENSA, suggested Herbert might take out a show similar to the one we had recently done in Canada. Herbert produced and compèred it. The forces were grand audiences and sharing in their discomforts, living in make-shift accommodation, changing costumes in lavatories and draughty passages made one feel a part of the whole effort. I remember one particularly tense evening. We were playing at a sea-plane base near Devonport. We had been told that the men were coming in from a raid and that we could not start the performance until they were safely down, because every available light was needed to guide them.

It soon became evident that one of the aircraft was missing. We were very conscious of the tension building up as the minutes passed.

We started the show eventually, feeling unhappy about the obvious anxiety. Then suddenly a message came from the C.O., asking us to call a halt. Immediately the hall was plunged into darkness. Here and there a tiny point of light sprang from the blackness as torches used by the audience were switched on and focused on the stage. Billy Milton kept things going with his songs and light-hearted patter. He seemed to know just how to adapt himself to each and every audience. The air was thick with speculation. Then someone peered through a corner of the black-out and a whisper ran round the hall – the flarepath lights were on! It could mean only one thing. The missing plane was limping home . . . ! We all ended that evening feeling slightly drunk, not on alcohol, but relief and happiness. It was round about now that I first met that 'female Peter Pan' of singers, Vera Lynn – one of the truly *nicest*, talented and most unspoiled stage personalities I know. All she had to do was stand there and sing to become, and remain, the 'Forces' Sweetheart' through three decades. With reunion after reunion of El Alamein veterans we meet her looking barely a day older; her voice unimpaired, her gentle charm unchanged. A rare showbusiness phenomenon; so modest no one could even envy her – only admire and respect her.

After the ENSA tour, Robert Donat asked me to do a play: Jane Austen's *Emma*. I was thrilled. I had always adored Jane's novels and jumped at the chance of playing one of her heroines. It seemed to me, too, perfect escapist entertainment. For a couple of hours, anyway, our audiences could leave behind the horrors of the mid-20th century for the leisurely calm of the early 19th. It was a superb production Robert put on, designed by Gladys Calthrop.

At the top right-hand corner of the page of sketches illustrating the lovely dresses designed by Gladys Calthrop, you will see a simple white dress, no touch of colour except a garnet pendant which picked up the light.

Nothing extraordinary about the dress at all – but every performance as I entered centre stage through the double doors of Emma's drawing room the audience spontaneously applauded.

Why was it? Why does an audience sometimes, for no

obvious reason, wish to show its appreciation? It does not often happen but when it does – it gives one such a glow of pleasure.

We were to do a three-month provincial tour with *Emma* beginning in Manchester, before opening in London in September. I was so happy in the part that we rechristened our home at Elstree '*Hartfield*,' the name of Emma's home.

Part-way through, in June, we heard the King's broadcast announcing the D-Day landings. We were jubilant, until the Nazis began their last fling with the doodle-bugs. In the circumstances Robert Donat decided to extend the tour until the danger to London was over.

The provinces loved *Emma*. They responded exactly as we had hoped: it was a very happy tour for me.

The V-1s were still hurtling down unpredictably when we returned to London, so our opening was further delayed, and in the interim Herbert decided to make what turned out to be the first of perhaps our most successful run of movies, later to be known as the 'London Series'. *I Live in Grosvenor Square* was a fairly serious film with a war-time theme: a triangle, with myself as a WAAF, engaged to an English Army Officer aboard, who meets and falls in love with an American pilot. Later in the film the American dies in a crash deliberately engineered to avoid destroying a village (the village where, as it happened, my family lived).

We made the film at Dartington Hall in Devon amid glorious English scenery. Rex Harrison played my fiancé. He was superb. Altogether we had a fine cast, Robert Morley and the American, Dean Jagger, and the film was to do outstanding business. At one time it was running concurrently in two rival cinemas side-by-side. The old Empire and Warner's in Leicester Square.

Emma finally opened at the St James's Theatre around the beginning of February 1945. Very soon after we opened the second wave of doodle-bugs, the more deadly V-2s, began to arrive.

This was particularly sad as *Emma* was a perfect play for people coming in from the Home Counties. We had very early curtains especially to accommodate them. We rang up at six-fifteen, and the play was over by eight-thirty, so they could get home, at least much of the time, before the blackout. But there is no doubt that the V-2s were bad for business.

One matinee, when the theatre was packed with ladies (mainly elderly), there was a tremendous crash, as it seemed, either inside, or immediately outside the theatre. Everything rocked.

Mr Weston, one of the characters in the play, burst on to the stage crying, 'Oh, a terrible thing has happened, my love.'

'What is it, my love?' his wife asked in alarm.

'A catastrophe. Someone has broken into the turkey house. Not a turkey left!'

A momentary pause and then – a roar of laughter swept through the audience. We learned later that a V-2 had actually landed not very far from the theatre in Piccadilly and that we had, in fact, had a lucky escape. It was *Emma*'s death knell.

I learned so much on this extensive tour of *Emma* about the provincial theatre, which was to be repeated in the 1960s with a long tour with *Person Unknown*. That so very many theatres are being demolished to make way for office blocks, is, I think, a sad state of affairs. Obviously the large old theatres can't be sustained but I have in mind those comparable with the perfect Grand Theatre at Blackpool, the fate of which, as I write this, hangs in the balance. There is such a growing interest in theatre from both audiences and dedicated groups of writers, artistes and directors, but the time and money required to build new theatres make their efforts doubly difficult.

With the closure of *Emma* I was invited by Hugh (Binkie) Beaumont to join Rex Harrison and Roland Culver in a production of *French Without Tears*, which he was preparing for an ENSA tour on the Continent. I jumped at the idea. Acting with Rex had been one of the most exciting experiences of my career and he and 'Roly' Culver had played in *French Without Tears* when it was presented originally. It had been a landmark in recent theatrical history. It was an ideal light comedy, with only one set and a minimum of costume changes, so perfect for the problems of transport in the still pretty devastated countries we were to visit.

To go abroad we had to be uniformed and 'briefed'. Duly we arrived at the Theatre Royal, Drury Lane, their ENSA Headquarters.

The auditorium was stripped of almost all the seating, just a row or so left in the middle. We were a small company, so sat in a little group, awaiting the arrival of the Welfare Officer. We were given various instructions from the stage, which made me, at least, feel rather like a small school-girl. We were told to take care of our uniforms as they were the property of ENSA. If we had an accident with them to report it immediately to our hostel superintendent. We were to take no more than two suitcases, one for our costumes and one for personal belongings. And to make sure that the labels all bore our company number. Someone put up a hand to ask a question: 'Please, what is our company number?'

'You don't *know*? Why you've been XYZ to me for weeks.' I can still see Rex's face and hear him mutter 'XYZ not NBG?' Rex is, I would say, the most truly sophisticated person I've ever met as well as the most brilliant actor I've worked with.

We flew from Croydon to Brussels, European headquarters of ENSA. Plans for our first 'date' had not been set, so we went to the hostel, a small but very comfortable hotel and awaited developments. That night we learned that we were to go to Eindhoven. The troops were moving into Germany but there were still quite a number there and it would be better than doing nothing. We agreed.

How those men enjoyed that show! And I must pay tribute to the FANY drivers who got us to Eindhoven. Roads were, of course, in an appalling state, but not once on the tour did a car or van break down.

It was sad to see the state of the people at Eindhoven. The thin children, the women with sunken eyes. Also it was something of a shock to find we weren't welcomed with open arms. They were quite indifferent to us. Until seeing the devastation of parts of the town I'm afraid I'd not realised that these people had not only suffered the occupation with all its terrifying implications but had night after night suffered bombings from allied planes.

I'm ashamed now of our lack of sensitivity when some of us went into an open-air café. We were in the end served with something or other, but grudgingly. The Dutch had been quite literally starving and there was still very little food; the shops empty of anything. They knew in that little café that we were at a hostel (ours, incidentally, had been a Luftwaffe brothel) and well provided with food by the NAAFI. Of course, the Dutch were thankful for liberation, but the suffering was still there.

This first experience made me very aware of the remarkable efficiency with which our own rationing system had functioned. We ourselves, living at Elstree, with vegetables from the garden and eggs from a few chickens, had indeed been in comparative clover.

We had hoped to go on into Germany, feeling the show would be so perfect for the troops there, but instead were sent to Ostend. Although the war was virtually over there were still masses of barbed wires and warnings of mines on the beaches. There were thousands of prisoners of war waiting to be sent 'home' and at Eindhoven, a dispersal centre for those newly released from the concentration camps. The medical C.O. told us he doubted more than a minority of the victims would ever recover their health. It is to the care of so many of these unfortunate people that Sue Ryder has dedicated her life.

At Ostend we visited a hospital. In one bed was an elderly man apparently a seaman who had been picked up from the sea. The Matron wondered if perhaps I could 'get through to him'. They had no idea as to his identity and he was not expected to survive much longer. They didn't even know his nationality but thought he was probably English. I tried, but there was not even a flicker of response. At Brussels there was a similar experience. I visited Mlle Bihet at the Marie Depage–Edith Cavell Institute. By now this was a vast hospital which had trained thousands of nurses. How proud Miss Cavell would have been had she lived to see it. But in one room was a man lying quite motionless. On a chair by his bed lay his concentration camp clothes. No-one knew who he was, or where he was from. There was little anyone could do but how one's heart ached for the victims of all this misery.

With Bebe Daniels and Ben Lyon, back in 1941, Herbert and I had gone to East Grinstead where Archie MacIndoe was performing miracles of plastic surgery. I know we all felt completely inadequate, giving a light-hearted performance for these mainly young men of the R.A.F. Some of the children, men and women who had been seriously hurt in air raids would, without the skill of MacIndoe and his colleagues, have remained disfigured for life.

On a much happier note was the week in Paris. We played at the Marigny Theatre and were put up at a little Pension close to the Opéra Comique. The Old Vic Company was playing at the Comédie Française. We all ate together at a long table: Laurence Olivier, Ralph Richardson, Joyce Redman, Margaret Leighton and darling, darling Sybil Thorndike, throwing off enthusiasm like sparks.

I remember beautiful Maggie dashing in one day. She had found some pretty ear-rings and the delight of Sybil as she admired them on Maggie . . . These ear-rings were the sort of clever thing the French people had managed to do – with nothing. I got some myself later. I don't really know what they were made of, but they were very effective and I'm sure this sort of ingenuity had helped the French girls keep up their reputation for elegance which was commented upon by our press at home when reporting on Paris as the liberating forces moved in.

When at the General Election in 1945 the Churchill Government was overthrown, Herbert was staggered. I was too; I thought I understood the reason why Sir Winston was an inspiration to all of us and his magnificent leadership was without doubt instrumental in saving us from the terrible experiences of some of the allied countries. But by 1945 the forces felt the war was behind them. Meeting and talking with so many on the ENSA tour, I'd come to the conclusion they were completely 'browned off'. Many had come straight from the fighting in Burma to the fighting in France without getting home on any leave at all. There wasn't any more fighting and they just couldn't see why they weren't getting back to civvy street immediately. I'm quite certain there were many valid reasons for the necessity of keeping them in Europe. But to them, they were wasting valuable time in taking up their normal lives again. So they were mostly utterly disillusioned.

With the war over, actors and actresses returned to their jobs.

Looking back I still marvel that the film studios managed not only to make films during the difficult times of shortages, black-out and transport problems, but for the British film industry to take so many strides forward through those years. (One has only to remember Noël Coward's *In Which We Serve*, to appreciate the achievement.)

After *Grosvenor Square* Herbert planned another London story: *Piccadilly Incident*. We had hoped to sign up Rex Harrison again, but by now Rex had a Hollywood contract and was lost to us. Herbert approached John Mills. He was not available either.

An agent, Eric Goodhead, had persistently telephoned Herbert while we were making *They Flew Alone* about a young actor named Michael Wilding. Michael had at that time done a little revue work and a few plays, including *Quiet Weekend*. We had seen him, but he had made little impact on us. His agent, still persistent, suggested him for *Piccadilly Incident* and offered to show us a film clip of Michael's work. We saw it. We were still not very impressed. He was *all right*, but hardly co-starring material. Herbert invited him to dinner at Claridges. We found him charming, delightful, diffident – but was this enough? Since everyone else we wanted was otherwise engaged, we took a chance.

Throughout the first day's shooting I found myself constantly comparing him in my mind with Rex. Poor Michael! He was nervous enough to begin with and sensitive enough, I'm sure, to feel my resistance.

Then, on the second day, something very strange happened: something I find difficult to explain. In a not-particularly-important scene Michael performed some small, instinctive 'piece of business' which made me blink and mentally sit up.

That evening I asked Herbert: 'D'you think he's as good as I do?'

'Better,' said Herbert.

And so was born, in the words of Godfrey Winn, 'The

greatest team in British films, and what is so nice, they're our sort of people, not so-called glamour stars, but good hard working professionals – laughing, dancing and romancing together.' Nothing could have pleased Michael or me more than Godfrey's tribute.

The 'London Series' as it was called resulted from a casual meeting during our customary Sunday morning walk. It was at Gerards Cross. We saw approaching us our good friend Maurice Cowan, for many years the editor of *The Picturegoer*. Maurice started what was known as *The Picturegoer* Award for the best Actor and Actress of the Year, which I had won. 'I've got a good story for you, Herbert,' he said – 'I Live in Grosvenor Square' – he briefly described it. 'It's mine,' said Herbert. It was a very great success. Then followed *Piccadilly Incident*, *The Courtneys of Curzon Street*, *Spring in Park Lane* and *Maytime in Mayfair*. All of these stemmed from that accidental meeting with Maurice Cowan.

Maurice must also be given full credit for the TV series *The Six Wives of Henry VIII*. He sent Herbert the script but he was too involved on another project. But he did tell Maurice he thought the idea was a goldmine. Maurice, I thought, was not given sufficient credit for his second successful series. He, together with his charming wife Lore, were a wonderful writing team – and lovable friends. Maurice, alas, died quite recently.

The impact of the 'London Series' on the British film industry was far more important than the records of box-office receipts of £1,600,000 on *Spring in Park Lane* alone. This was, of course, when the price of admission was much lower than it is today, and the attendance record can never be beaten, since *Spring* played in most of the 5,200 cinemas that then existed, of which only about 1,700 remain in existence today.

Piccadilly Incident was rather a sad story, but it had a sort of magic about it; and two of the ingredients of the magic were Michael and me. We just welded. Our chemistry was right. Even the critics were unanimous. We had made a great hit. Herbert won the *Daily Mail* National Film Award for the best film of the year; I won the *Picturegoer* Gold Medal Annual Award for the second time, and started six consecutive years as top British film actress. I was, by one newspaper, awarded the unofficial title of 'First Lady of the British Screen'. And it was, of course, the start of Michael's career as a star. Herbert hastily signed him on a long contract!

Piccadilly Incident went on General Release as we started the third London film, *The Courtneys of Curzon Street*, and there were long queues for it everywhere.

The Courtneys, a sort of family saga, was even bigger. It was beautifully dressed, there was a lot of sentiment and some lovely dances; the sort of film for the whole family which is so rarely made today.

I had a very interesting experience indeed connected with the marriage of Princess Elizabeth and Prince Philip. I was invited to speak the narration for the *Pathé Gazette* short film of the event. This meant going to a studio in Wardour Street when the film had been assembled to record, and this included speaking the words of the marriage vows, since recording was not permitted in the Abbey at that time.

A special private viewing was arranged for Queen Mary. I was invited to sit next to her. She sat bolt upright, first through a showing of *Scrapbook for 1922*, which must have stirred many sad memories for her, showing as it did her dead husband and the then Prince of Wales, her exiled son; this was followed by the wedding film. It was not until the words of the solemn dedication to each other of the young Prince and Princess were spoken that she touched her eyes with a handkerchief.

When the scenes in Buckingham Palace came on, it was obvious that the Royal party was experiencing difficulty in controlling the younger members for the formal family photographs. Queen Mary turned to me. 'The children were getting so tired – and so *tiresome*, by then,' she remarked. Then, as she left, 'You spoke your words very well. Did you have a good view of the wedding?'

'Oh no, Ma'am,' I replied, 'I was not there.'

'Not there. Oh! You poor thing,' she said. 'What a pity.'

Then came the biggest hit of all: *Spring in Park Lane*. No poignancy this time: light, life, gaiety and fun. The story was based on Alice Duer Miller's *Come Out of the Pantry*. Herbert changed it a good deal, but the basic story was there. It was a lovely, light, glamorous comedy with, apart from Michael and me, Peter Graves, Nicholas Phipps, Tom Walls from the Aldwych farces, and Nigel Patrick, in the early stages of his very successful career. It was the sort of film Herbert loved to make. It was while we were making a Personal Appearance tour with it that he made his remark to Michael about the people who lived in drab little houses in industrial towns. This was the sort of film we made for them.

Spring was Michael's first 'dancing' film. During the making of *Courtneys*, I was practising a 'lift' with Terry Kendall (father of enchanting, but tragic Kay Kendall who was to die all too soon from leukaemia).

Michael came on to the set, watched for a moment, then put his arm around me and remarked off-handedly: 'I can do that.' And he did! I'd no idea he could dance. He still insists that he can't. But he did. The 'dream' dance, to the music of *The Moment I Saw You* was one of the most enjoyable sequences in the film.

After *Spring in Park Lane* Michael went off to make *An Ideal Husband* with Korda and I made a film without him: *Elizabeth of Ladymead*. It was a fascinating exercise: I played four different characters, all women left behind while their husbands went off to war: Beth's to the Crimea, Elizabeth's to South Africa, Betty's to the First World War and Liz's to the Second.

Each character was different, and differently affected by the separation. The constant factor in the story was the house: *Ladymead*.

It gave me tremendous scope, and I enjoyed it. I think perhaps it was a little ahead of its time. It had a touch of Women's Lib. about it in places! Or perhaps the public was disappointed that, although I played with four excellent leading men, Michael and I were not together again. Or – who knows? There are a hundred reasons why a book, play, film or television series is a success or a disappointment. Only rarely can a finger be put squarely on the reason.

If it was the absence of Michael we made this good in the next, and last, 'London' film: *Maytime in Mayfair*, in which I played the Directress of a famous Fashion House. Dior's 'New Look' had been sensational. Now another 'look' was in – hems shot down from the knee almost to the ankle. It was a terrible headache. The film would not be issued for six months, perhaps a year. Goodness knows what would have happened to fashions by then. If women rejected the new hemline it could be disastrous. I still wince when I come across any of the stills. Women *did* reject it but it didn't affect the appeal of the film. *Maytime in Mayfair* was a huge success. It didn't quiet reach the heights of *Spring in Park Lane*, but we certainly had nothing to complain about. We seemed to be riding on a rainbow. Nothing we did could go very far wrong. Wherever we went there were smiling crowds. When we did a Personal Appearance at Worthing the crowds began to line our route a mile outside the town. When we arrived at the cinema we almost literally had to fight our way in. It was the equivalent, I suppose, of a present-day Pop Group welcome. Michael, bless him, positively refused to make a speech.

When I called him on-stage after the show to take a bow he just walked up to me and kissed me, and the audience went *mad*.

1949 was a tremendously busy and very exciting year for us all. Michael, Herbert and I won National Film Awards for *Spring in Park Lane*; and Laurence Olivier and I won the *Picturegoer* Gold Medal Award, each of us for the fourth time.

At one of the Royal Film Performances, which is held each year for the Cinematograph Trades Benevolent Fund, I was asked to make the speech of thanks to the King at the end of the evening.

Later we were all presented to the Royal pair.

Because Michael, Herbert and I had surnames beginning with 'W' we stood in the presentation line together. Under the 'Ts', close by, was Elizabeth Taylor. She looked stunningly beautiful, with those truly violet-coloured eyes and (most unfairly to the rest of us) a *double* row of natural black eyelashes! Michael could hardly keep his eyes away from her and I noticed with amusement that the attraction was mutual. Elizabeth was already attracted to Michael, I believe. She had been working in the same studios as ourselves not long before, and positively haunted our stage. She was only about sixteen then, and frequently suffered the indignity of being called away to get on with her school work. She really was gorgeous though lacking, I think, the sensitive beauty which enhanced Vivien Leigh's loveliness. Vivien had the most perfect face I have ever seen.

Herbert and I went to the States to promote the London series. Returning, I learned that Alan's ship was due at Dunkirk. After six years back in the Royal Navy he'd found he couldn't adjust to civilian life again and was with a South African shipping-line. As I'd not seen him for twenty-two years Herbert agreed to take me over – 'Book a suite in the best hotel,' he told a travel agent. 'Suite,' said the astonished man, 'I'll be lucky if I can find an hotel!'

We were a little puzzled until we reached Calais. I had seen war devastation during my ENSA tour, but *nothing* like this. The whole of the northern coast of France, four years after the war ended, was a wasteland. We did in the end find a tiny room in an *auberge* near Dunkirk. There were still bullet holes in the walls.

The reunion with Alan was joyful. I found Alan had changed very little. As Herbert had to get back to London I spent a few days aboard the ship – a happy, nostalgic time. After that there were occasional leaves in England, and in 1964 we spent Christmas with him at Malta. Sadly his wife, whom I never met, had died some time earlier, so when he retired in 1965 he settled back in England.

It was the disclosure of the *Spring in Park Lane* figures in the House of Commons, which led to Harold Wilson, then President of the Board of Trade, getting together with Sir Arthur Jarratt, head of British Lion and Sir Wilfred Eady of the Treasury, to work out a plan whereby the Producer received more of the box-office takings. What is now known as the Eady plan or British Film Production Fund emerged and it has been of enormous help to producers.

The Courtneys of Curzon Street was largely responsible for bringing Harold Drayton and his powerful city associates into British Lion. This was one of my brief and rare excursions into financial circles, which culminated at a supper party given by Sir Arthur Jarratt, to eminent bankers, financiers, who all looked the part of former city magnates – except one.

He looked like a real Yeoman farmer from the Shires and strangely out of key with the rest of the company. He was Harold Drayton – head of the B.E.T. and one of the great financiers of the past 20 years. But on appearance, he was miscast. In private life he lived up to his looks and his home at Plumpton near Bury St Edmunds with its enormous farm and his lovely collection of old books – his hobby – put him fairly and squarely where he should be.

Herbert had a cold when we stayed with Harley and Chris and it was quite something to see this financial genius putting a poker in a blazing log fire and then into a jug of claret. 'Nothing like mulled Claret for a cold, Anna,' he said, 'try some.' I did, it was awful. But by the morning, Herbert's cold was cured.

Herbert won National Film Awards in succession for the best British Film of the Year with *Piccadilly Incident, Courtneys of Curzon Street* and *Spring in Park Lane* and, the following year, won it with *Odette*, bringing our joint awards up to thirteen.

A trip we made to New York at this time was, I think, our last by sea. We were to join the *Queen Elizabeth* at Cherbourg but rough weather prevented her getting into harbour and we had to spend the night at a small dockside hotel. The Duke of Windsor was also bound for New York. The next morning coffee and rolls were served in a sort of shed, with all queuing up – no special priority for H.R.H. During the crossing Herbert and I were invited to dine with him. There was one other woman besides myself but, apparently she didn't dance – the Duke held out his hand to me and we had a delightful time on the dance floor as he was an exceptionally good dancer. 'The Duchess,' he told me 'has a new Rumba step – unusual and interesting rythm – like to try it?' Of course I would. I trod all over his feet. I apologised explaining that I couldn't quite find the beat. He laughed. 'Let's try again,' he suggested. We did. He trod on my feet. We both laughed and he led me back to the table. 'Difficult,' he said, 'but thanks for trying.' No wonder they'd called him the Prince Charming.

Chapter Sixteen

A ND now a major event in my life – *Odette*. The following citation appeared in the *London Gazette* on Friday, August 16th 1946:

'The King has been graciously pleased to award the George Cross to:
Odette Marie Celine, Mrs Sansom, M.B.E., Women's Training Services (First Aid Nursing Yeomanry). Mrs Sansom was infiltrated into enemy occupied France and worked with great courage and distinction until April 1943 when she was arrested with her Commanding Officer. In addition the Gestapo were most determined to discover the whereabouts of a wireless operator and of another British officer whose lives were of the greatest value to the Resistance Organisation. Mrs Sansom was the only person who knew of their whereabouts. The Gestapo tortured her most cruelly to try to make her give away this information. They seared her back with a red hot iron and when that failed they pulled out all her toenails. Mrs Sansom, however, continually refused to speak and by her bravery and determination she not only saved the lives of the two officers but also enabled them to carry on their most valuable work. During the period of over two years in which she was in enemy hands she displayed courage, endurance and self sacrifice of the highest possible order.'

What the citation does not mention is that after her interrogation and torture in Paris Odette spent the rest of the

War years in Ravensbrück women's prison in Germany where she endured the most appalling privation and barely escaped with her life. The other women who were captured with her either died or were executed.

Another thing not mentioned is that before she was gently pressured into carrying out her dangerous mission Odette was merely a housewife and mother of three girls. She gave permission to the War Office to tell her full story and when it was written guaranteed its authenticity. Odette added in her own words a short note, 'It is with a sense of deep humility that I allow my personal story to be told. My comrades who did far more than I and suffered far more profoundly are not here to speak. Because of this I speak for them and I would like this book to be a window through which may be seen those very gallant women with whom I had the honour to serve.'

Like many other people I had no knowledge until I read the story of Odette's George Cross award in the newspapers that there were a few women, 38 in all, who had been infiltrated into France as contacts between the British and the French Resistance movement. It was perhaps a year later that I received the manuscript of the book with the suggestion that Herbert might like to make a film of Odette's experiences. I knew after reading it that this was no rôle for me. I felt no actress, except one who had experienced something of the menace of living in an occupied country under the constant fear of informers, could get inside the heart and mind of Odette. However, Herbert bought the film rights of the book and went to Hollywood and endeavoured to persuade Ingrid Bergman to play Odette. She read the book and turned it down. 'It is too sad – too grim – no-one would pay to see such a film.' Herbert approached Michele Morgan who also turned it down. Later, during the filming of *Maytime in Mayfair* with Michael Wilding Herbert told me at lunch break that we were to have visitors later that day. Jerard Tickell, the author of the book, Odette, and Peter Churchill, her Commanding Officer in France. I cannot begin to describe my feelings when I saw this fragile looking girl, with her extraordinary lustrous and penetrating eyes. I was stunned. I had made quite clear to Herbert and with finality that I would not consider playing Odette's part in a film. Now it appeared that this visit was arranged in order to change my mind. Odette herself asked me to reconsider my decision. Offers from other companies to buy the story were pouring in from Hollywood as well as England. There was no doubt that the film would be made. The three closest to the story were anxious that it should be made in Britain and Odette herself was most anxious that I should play her part. Still I hesitated. I had played a number of 'real' people in films, one of whom, at least, had died as a victim of war. But this was different. Odette still lived. She was an historical character and in some respects she had endured more, physically and mentally, even than Nurse Cavell. I felt I was not equipped to portray her. Finally a lunch party was arranged which included Colonel Maurice Buckmaster, Commanding Officer of the Special Operations Executive, French Section, the man who had masterminded the whole operation of Odette. During lunch he turned to me and said quite calmly, 'Anna, I do hope you are going to play Odette. I am sure you will do her justice.' 'You must play it, Anna,' added Odette.

So that was that. Although I'm sure neither Odette nor Peter would wish it to be noised abroad, both made it a condition that they would not accept any compensation for their story or invaluable contribution to the production.

In some ways, though infinitely more harrowing, my research for this part was easier than for many others, since the people who had lived the story were constantly with me, travelling to the places where they had worked and suffered, explaining what they had done, describing their emotions at different stages. With them we went to the Côte d'Azur which in their day had been in the unoccupied zone, but under surveillance of the Vichy police and Gestapo. We saw the spots on the coast where they had made their secret landings. Peter Churchill's was by submarine at St Christophe. The last time we saw Peter before he died we went with him to see the plaque in the red rocks at St Christophe commemorating his first arrival. The plaque read:

'Captain Peter Churchill, D.S.O., Croix de Guerre, landed here alone in the night, January 1942.'

I remember Peter saying to me, 'Men doing this was part of the job – it was the women who had guts.'

Odette herself landed in France by felucca from Gibraltar to Cassis near Marseilles. Inland we visited the towns and villages where they had worked with the Resistance at Arles and St Jorioz, Faverges, the tiny village in the Haute Savoie close to the spot where the French maquis was first organised – we stayed at the small Hotel de la Poste which had been their final headquarters and which was still run by the young couple who had been there throughout the occupation and who had hidden agents at the risk of torture and death. In those days they had tramped through the snow delivering messages, but regarded all this as nothing. With Odette and Peter we met other people they had known in the dark days who through the grapevine heard of their arrest and believed them long since dead. The sight of these reunions are amongst the most joyous yet at the same time most poignant experiences of my life. The more I saw and heard the more I realised that this film must be made but my overwhelming reluctance remained and never left me. The worst part of our journey was yet to come.

We went to Paris.

I remember the first night Odette and Peter saying they wanted to take a short walk alone. Herbert and I waited in an open air café. We knew our friends were steeling themselves to visit the site of some of Odette's most appalling suffering. We met by arrangement a little later outside the Gestapo headquarters at 84 Avenue Foch. It was a very sombre evening. I don't think any of us slept that night. The next day we went to Fresnes prison and visited the two cells, Peter's and Odette's. The walls were covered with script messages, crosses, initials, scraps of quotations from the Bible (all of them oddly hopeful). Odette pointed out the inscription she herself had left as a tiny memorial of her stay there. Just before we left Fresnes prison Odette asked the governor, 'Did they ever pick up "X"?', she mentioned the name of the stool pigeon who had betrayed them. 'If you look up on the landing above,' replied the governor, 'you will see him looking down at you now – he believes you to be dead.' Odette glanced swiftly upwards, then turned away.

Twelve times Odette was taken from Fresnes for interrogation at the Avenue Foch. A 45-minute drive in a black maria. A little cell on wheels over roughly cobbled and pot-holed streets, never knowing what lay at the end of the journey. It is a mental torture. We made the same journey in the same way so that I could to some tiny degree identify myself with her feelings. When we arrived at 84 Avenue Foch we found the main drawing-room floor on which Odette had been sentenced to death was now occupied by a very elegant, effeminate young man, apparently unaffected by the ghosts which must surely haunt the place. Higher still among what had obviously been servants' quarters was a labyrinth of tiny rooms with little skylights. These were the waiting rooms and close by were the torture rooms. Again there were initials and dates scratched on the walls, pathetic last attempts to send messages to the outside world and to friends and relatives.

Only twice in my presence did Odette lose her outward poise and tranquillity. In the room on the front of Avenue Foch where she was tortured she told us how she remembered hearing the voices of children playing far down in the Bois below. The sound of traffic, the sounds of everyday normal life. We stood back while she moved down the marvellous marble staircase which she had once before descended, her toenails torn out. Even then it was not simply her own memories which upset her. Afterwards she confessed that she could not bear having me suffer so because of her experiences. Later when we filmed the scenes of the torture at the studios she was terribly distressed and Herbert suggested she go to her room and rest. 'It is not for myself I am sad,' said Odette. 'I cannot bear to see Anna go through this.'

When the Nazis realised that nothing would make her talk she was sentenced to death. They sent her from Fresnes to the notorious Ravensbrück camp. Peter Churchill was sent to Saxenhausen, the fortress prison for VIPs (since Odette had persuaded the Nazis of Peter's relationship to Churchill). From here, towards the end of the war, these 'Hostage' prisoners were moved three hundred miles from camp to camp including Dachau: many were to die en route.

At Ravensbrück Odette was put into solitary confinement in complete darkness, and when the allies landed in the south of France she was kept without food for days, it being known it was she who had got the plans of Marseilles back to England – one of her first assignments.

I lived through the making of the film in a dazed anguish. The atmosphere was so authentic I sometimes felt for the first time that although I was not Odette I was no longer truly myself. The fact that I wore the clothes Odette had worn during her imprisonment helped this illusion of stifling my own personality. Herbert collected together a quite remarkable cast. Trevor Howard played Peter, Peter Ustinov played Arnaud, the radio operator, and Marius Goring the German Intelligence Officer who arrested Peter and Odette. There was (to me) genuine menace in his playing, very cold, very penetrating. Sometimes his eyes turned almost opaque.

The Interrogator too was terrifyingly lifelike. I felt real fear when confronting him. We heard later that he had been unhappy during the making of the film, having the impression that none of us liked him as a person. We did not. That was merely a compliment to his acting. We also learned later that he had been a genuine interrogator during the war – but on our side. I sometimes think that during the weeks of shooting it was Peter Ustinov, that great bundle of brilliance, who kept us all sane. Whenever we finished a tense scene we would go to Herbert's office for a break. Odette, Peter Churchill, Herbert, Marius Goring, Peter Ustinov and myself. Somehow Peter managed to shrug off his rôle more simply than the rest of us, and it was his fund of anecdotes, impersonations and stories which lifted us out of that almost unbearable tension. Trevor Howard played the part of Peter Churchill magnificently, though for me a little disconcertingly. Usually I am very aware of the give and take between screen partners during the playing of a scene. With Trevor I did not get this feeling. It was only when I saw the results on the screen that I realised what a truly remarkable performance his was for depth of feeling and expression. This was acting 'from the inside' with a vengeance. For me the most taxing scene of all immediately preceded the arrest of Odette and Peter. Peter, after a visit to England, was due to return and be dropped from a parachute on a nearby 6,000 foot mountain summit, the Semnoz. I and the radio officer, Arnaud, had to arrange a signal to show him where he could safely land. This meant lugging a heavy load of wood to the summit to make a bonfire. A very exhausting operation which could not be faked. Then, on Peter's arrival, there was one short but very important night shot which could only be taken once because it involved my crossing a bit of virgin sonw, which, once crossed, betrayed footmarks which would be left behind. A pit was dug for the camera so that this scene could be shot from below to give more dramatic impact. I had two short steep rushes uphill. The first to light the bonfire as a signal, the second to greet Peter as he landed. I was by now not only tired, my nerves were as taut as fiddle strings. During the second uphill rush I veered from my course and crashed into the camera pit, hurting my back and injuring my shoulder. Nothing to what Odette had suffered but bad enough at the time. By the end of the film I was feeling emotionally and physically exhausted.

However, the number of letters I received after the film première soon made me forget my exhaustion. Of these I would like to let you see extracts from four which were significant and gave me infinite pleasure.

FROM ODETTE'S DAUGHTERS – aged fifteen, thirteen and ten:

'It is difficult to find the right words to express what my sisters and I felt after having seen the film. We all felt that we wanted to be alone so that we could think over what we had just seen – So long as we live we shall never forget *Odette* – how wonderfully you became our Mummy – With love from the three of us –

Françoise, Lili and Marianne.'

COLONEL MAURICE BUCKMASTER – Commanding Officer S.O.E. French Section:

'Before any of my impressions of the film fade, I want to tell you that I had never imagined that anyone could produce as you have done, with the utmost fidelity and startling truthfulness, the experiences and feelings which must have been Odette's.'

NOËL COWARD:

'This is just to tell you I saw *Odette* last night and thought it one of the best acted and best directed pictures I have seen in many a long day – Your complete lack of compromise, your sincerity and veracity, impressed me very deeply.'

SYDNEY CARROLL, SUNDAY TIMES:

'In this film, dear Anna, you have reached a degree of tragic sublimity which puts all the artificial glamour of Hollywood to shame.

'I am one of the most hard-boiled of critics. One of the most difficult to please, because I have had the privilege of seeing all the greatest English speaking artistes of the last half century. Your performance in *Odette* moved me to tears. Tears of compassion; tears of resentment; tears of sympathy. I doubt if film acting has ever reached such a height, such a veracity of interpretation before.

Sincerely yours,
Sydney Carroll'

The Monarch, in those days, except for the annual Royal Film Performance in aid of the Cinematograph Trade Benevolent Fund, did not attend film premières, but, knowing the King had made an exception to attend Olivier's *Hamlet*, Herbert approached the appropriate authority. The King agreed but added to Lord Cromer, 'It's not going to be too harrowing, I hope.' Another night to remember at the Plaza Theatre, June 6th 1950. The whole of Lower Regent Street packed with crowds and all traffic diverted. As the film ended a 'thunderous silence' fell over the audience. No-one applauded. Minutes on end seemed to pass. I was stunned. It seemed we had failed. Then came the deafening applause which seemed to go on even longer than the silence. As was the custom we had been presented to the Royal party before the film began, but the Lord Chamberlain, Lord Cromer, came to us and told us the King and Queen would like to meet us again.

With Odette and Peter we waited. The Queen approached Odette. 'Thank you for allowing your story to be told.' And to me she said simply, 'Thank you for having portrayed Odette so sincerely.' The King said to Peter, with his eyes on Odette, 'She looks beautiful. How much can the spirit stand before the flesh breaks.' This must have been prophetic since at this time he knew he was yet another victim of malignant cancer. A few weeks after the première we were invited to the Garden Party at Buckingham Palace. We were singled out for a few words with the King. He shook hands and said to me, 'It must have been a great strain playing Odette. I hope you have quite recovered.' He then went on to say, 'I can understand that in the theatre you can build up a crisis scene, but how can you do some of these scenes out of continuity? The whole thing must be like a jigsaw puzzle. How can you possibly arrive, say, on the Monday morning and play a torture scene "cold"?' It was a most perceptive question. He could not have known it but something like this actually did happen. Long before I had worked my way into the character of Odette – in fact on the second day's shooting – I had to play one of the very last scenes of all in which Odette returned from Ravensbrück to be questioned by her Commanding Officer, Maurice Buckmaster. Luckily Colonel Buckmaster played the part himself, which was some help. I felt quite desperate during the rehearsal. Odette was waiting. We filmed the scene, then Odette came across and asked Buckmaster, 'How did you feel about that?' Maurice replied, 'It gave me precisely the same feeling when you came into the room.' Odette nodded. Perhaps that very feeling of

despair which imbued me helped to create the sense of empti-
ness Odette must have felt at the time.

The King continued his 'interrogation'. 'What happens if
you arrive at the studio one morning and feel you cannot play
a scene?' Herbert chipped in here. 'They must discipline
themselves, Sir. It's like any other job of work.' The King
laughed and turned to me, 'He's a hard taskmaster, eh?' 'Oh,
no,' I replied, 'he's most understanding and patient.'

Premières at all the capital cities in Europe which had been
occupied (other than those behind the Iron Curtain) were
arranged and invariably honoured by the presence of the
heads of state. Odette and Peter were with us on all these
occasions. Odette's mother, with her French logic, was giving
Odette some advice. Odette's three daughters were listening.
'Your most difficult time,' said mama, 'will be in Paris. After
all, you are French, and France is where it all happened, so
you are sure to have a very warm welcome. If they are very
enthusiastic stand still and wait for the applause to die down
before you speak.' Odette's little daughter chipped in, 'Don't
count too much on that, Mummy.' But it happened exactly as
Odette's mother predicted. Another never to be forgotten
occasion.

The Guard Republicaine lined the steps of the opera-house.
President Auriol graced the proceedings with his presence.
When we arrived the band struck up the Marseillaise and at the
end of the picture Odette walked onto the stage. Led by the
President the entire audience rose as one and gave her a storm-
ing wave of applause. Her speech ended, Odette walked to the
wings and led me on. After my few words we were taken
to the President's box. He could not have been more cordial
or enthusiastic. We had been warned beforehand that no
photographers would be allowed near the President's box,
so I was greatly surprised when I heard the President say to
Odette, 'I am afraid some photographers are here, do you

mind?' This was the climax. Odette, a French woman, being acclaimed in Paris for a great chapter in French history. The next day we were present to see her made Chevalier of the Legion d'Honneur at the Chancillerie.

Odette, I am happy to say, remains one of my closest friends. Now very happily married to Geoffrey Hallowes, she lives in London within easy calling distance of her family, her three daughters and six grandchildren. Something of her terrible ordeal still shines through her eyes and physically it has left its mark, but her spirit is undamaged and illuminates everything she does. Her friendship is one of my most precious possessions. It was in a curious way to help me when I faced a very difficult crisis in my own life a few years later. It was typical of Odette when she was invested with the George Cross by King George VI that she said, 'Thank you, Sir. May I accept this on behalf of my friends who have not returned.'

The making of the film was a tremendous experience and I shall always be proud of the fact that following my portrayal of Odette I was appointed an Honorary Ensign of the FANY Corps and was quite recently made a Vice-President. At St Paul's, Knightsbridge, you will find a memorial shrine with the names of the FANYs who gave their lives carrying out their secret assignments and dying lone violent deaths. Never have I felt so angry as when I heard on the radio a report of a book denigrating their work and their courage. Odette, typically, had 'nothing to say', but received a public apology in the House of Commons. Peter received substantial damages and costs, settled out of court. Violette Szabo, posthumously awarded the George Cross and Croix de Guerre, was not here to speak. She was executed at Natsweiller concentration camp.

Chapter Seventeen

HAVING to travel from Elstree and working at Shepperton Studios with offices in Mount Street, put an extra strain on both Herbert and me – so we decided to sell Hartfield House and move to London.

Luck was certainly with us as the agent had a flat in Park Lane overlooking Hyde Park.

One inspection was sufficient. A balcony running the length of the flat with a view as far as Harrow-on-the-Hill to the right – Croydon to the left and the city dominated by the Dome of St Paul's from the back – and a perfect niche for my Bechstein. It was here that we started our collection of French Impressionists. I was at Eastbourne with my aunt having a quiet rest, Herbert being busy on production matters. One evening as usual he phoned me, but what he told me I could scarcely believe. I put down the receiver, said to my aunt, 'We must go back to London at once. Herbert's gone mad – he's bought a Renoir, a Utrillo and a Boudin.'

Of course the prices then were nothing compared to the present day. When I got home – there they were – on the walls and lit by picture lights. They looked beautiful.

Our friend the art dealer said Herbert had driven a hard bargain and we had a safe investment.

Fortified by this opinion, we added in quick succession a Van Gogh, Gauguin, Fantin-Latour, two Brueghels and a small portrait of his mistress Saskia by Rembrandt. Added to which we acquired a lovely bronze of a dancer by Degas, a bust by Renoir and a Henry Moore figure.

Our sculptures were unexpectedly augmented when one evening at the Caprice Restaurant a very distinguished-looking diner leaned over and said to Herbert, 'I'd like to do a bust of your lovely wife.' Herbert looked round. It was Epstein! They hadn't met since the days at the Café Royal. We were both delighted with the idea. It was an extraordinary experience. I arrived for my first session on a very cold day to find Epstein carrying a bucket of coke, his boots covered in snow. He'd just been clearing the snow from the roof, he told me, as he proceeded to stoke up the boiler in the corner of the big studio. Almost the whole of one wall was taken up with a magnificent work – a figure of the Madonna and Child, commissioned for a convent. Two members of the Order were due to see the finished work before it was delivered. They were ecstatic, as is everyone who sees it placed so superbly at the north side of Cavendish Square. There were busts of Shaw, and Einstein, which, even I, with little knowledge of this form of art, recognised as works of genius.

In all I had eleven sittings, each filled with interest as he would talk of his experiences and had that simplicity which characterises so many great artists. His wife would come in to discuss various domestic matters, the food she was preparing for their son, a talented painter, working in his own studio at Chelsea but whom she knew wouldn't eat at all unless she took the meal to him. Epstein seemed able to switch his mind in all directions without ever losing his concentration on the job he was engaged on. But, I sensed that things were not easy in the matter of finance. I told Herbert. The next sitting, Herbert came with me. He took Epstein aside. 'May I suggest something on account?' he asked. 'It would be a Godsend,' replied Epstein. 'I have many problems.' Herbert gave him a cheque. The dear man was transformed.

My sessions over, I knew there would be some while to wait for the work to be cast, so we were surprised and delighted when, answering a ring, there was Epstein himself clasping the bust in his arms. 'Come in,' said Herbert. 'Let me help you with that.' But Epstein hurriedly followed me into our living room, made straight for my dearest possession, the Bechstein, and pushed the heavy bust into position, inflicting a deep scar on the lid of the piano in the process. We pretended not to notice. He hesitated a moment then said, 'I'm sorry but would it be convenient –'

Herbert stopped him in his tracks, pulled out his cheque book and wrote a cheque. Epstein took it gladly, looked at it, and then at his work, and said, 'My happiest assignment.' It was not mine.

I have seen too much of inventive genius up against material pressure. Dear Walt Disney, if ever a genius came out of Hollywood – it was Walt. I recall when in Hollywood Herbert and I were invited by the financial backers to investigate one of Disney's films. It had run over budget and to them did not seem particularly good.

Should it be left unfinished and the investment written off? We saw the rough cut and at a certain point Herbert turned to the financial chief, 'That one tune makes your investment safe.'

It was *Wishing on a Star* and the film *Pinnocchio!* One of the greatest money makers of all time.

Again with Orson Welles. We had to sit through his 'rushes' of *Citizen Kane* at the studio every morning waiting to see our own 'rushes' of *Irene*. No-one at the studio seemed interested and I believe it had been mentally written off as unshowable. Herbert and I alone enthused and Orson has always remembered. Herbert was not slow in letting the RKO executives know our views. At the triumphant première at the El Capitan theatre Orson arrived late with John Barrymore. They must have had a good meal – they were noisy and full of high spirits. At the end of the film, which was enthusiastically received, Orson stood up in his seat and looked towards Herbert and me. 'You told me so,' he shouted in his foghorn voice.

In the pioneer days of television, Herbert and I once visited John Logie Baird, universally accepted as the inventor of TV, at his home – an old Victorian terrace house near the Crystal Palace. He was not well and we sat in his bedroom.

'Could a London première of a film be seen on TV at Manchester, Glasgow and Birmingham simultaneously?' asked Herbert.

'It could,' said Baird, with his delightful Scottish accent, 'but it would be costly.'

'How much?' asked Herbert. He knew it had never been done before.

'Three hundred and fifty pounds, maybe,' answered Baird. Herbert had expected a far higher figure.

'It's a deal,' said Herbert.

But the date of the première still found Baird in bed – ill, so it never happened.

The only one to support his old school friend with his crazy invention was Jack Buchanan, but even he, with his persuasive personality, could not find backing in the city.

Baird died without receiving either the credit, or cash, for his brain-child. After his death a fund was started for his widow. Knowing the enormous fortunes which have been made out of all aspects of television, I just hope she was finally adequately recompensed. The initial response was infinitesimal. Only last week we watched Peter Hall's magnificent production of *Figaro* on TV and recalled how Mozart was buried in a pauper's grave within a few years of the original presentation and, thus, never knew it was hailed as a classic.

The story behind the painting of our lovely Van Gogh – a red barge on the Seine – I was sorry to have heard, as it was often in my mind when I looked at the picture. This had been painted shortly before he left Paris for Arles. He was quite literally penniless and, although a frugal eater, had to eat to keep body and soul together. At a small bistro, the owner was a great admirer of his work and provided him with meals, telling him not to worry about payment until he sold some of his work. The bill soared to, in Van Gogh's eyes, an astronomical figure, the equivalent of a few pounds. So anxious did he become that he asked the kindly proprietor if he would accept one of his paintings in settlement. The owner agreed. That picture 'Barge on the Seine', for which Van Gogh received a few pounds' worth of food and drink, now hangs, we understand, in a Canadian art gallery, having been purchased for a vast sum.

These are some of the reasons why I say that my assignment with Epstein was not my happiest.

We had, in the opinion of our art dealers, one of the finest private collections of art in the country. Unfortunately circumstances were later to compel us to sell prematurely. Had we the same collection now we would be wealthy indeed. So Herbert was not so mad after all.

But that's all water under the bridge.

I had one regret about our new home – it was on the seventh floor, and I could not have a cat. Much too dangerous on the balcony and, no place to hunt, or trees to scratch.

Rufus was my last cat at Elstree – an offspring of one of the many kittens I'd distributed around the neighbouring area. He was quick-witted and highly intelligent. When we left Hartfield House, he remained with the new owners. I felt it was unfair to take him, accustomed to the country, into a seventh-floor London flat. But that balcony was a joy to my aunt who could sit and watch the activity below. She was really a Londoner and I don't think had ever completely resigned herself to the semi-country life of Elstree. From our bedroom window we could see the plaque on the wall in

South Street marking the place where Florence Nightingale had lived and died – and that gave us an idea!

Two of the most prized possessions in our home are a formal upright chair and a silver cigarette box. When we invite our friends to sit in the chair, which is often, they invariably look very surprised. It is a chair from Florence Nightingale's room at Lea Hurst in Derbyshire, perfect for posture – and comfort. The spine seems to fit into the uncomfortable looking back of the chair. When we were granted permission to film at Lea Hurst by Mr J. P. Mitchelhill, who with two friends had bought the house from the Nightingale family and formed a trust to make it a home of rest and convalescence for nurses – I was invited to sleep in Miss Nightingale's room. Never shall I forget the serenity. I was transported back to the time when she returned from the horrors of the Crimea to that small quiet bedroom with its magnificent views over the Derbyshire countryside. It was easy to envisage her looking from her balcony at the peaceful scene – reliving her terrible experiences – or perhaps, being Miss Nightingale, she was looking forward. I was allowed to see private letters and reading these in the very room from which so many of them emanated was an uncanny experience. It takes some time preparing for such rôles, but quite suddenly I was no longer reading or talking about Miss Nightingale, I was deeply aware of her, thinking of her and with her. She was alive in my brain and my imagination. Books written during her lifetime gave me little help, but this personal contact was inspirational and it became increasingly evident that the most immediately striking characteristic of Miss Nightingale was a deep religious belief that God had called upon her to dedicate her life to others and she was prepared to accept this responsibility. I was not able to meet many people who had actually known Miss Nightingale but there was a very old lady of the first trained army nurses who was a member of the original group sent to nurse British soldiers in China. She told me of the visit she and her six fellow nurses made to Miss Nightingale at 60 South Street the day before sailing. In her gentle manner Miss Nightingale wished the nurses Godspeed and the inspiration of her talk to them was something the old lady told us had remained with her for almost seventy years. She showed me with pride her grey and scarlet army uniform.

Is there one of us who has not pictured the lone, courageous Florence Nightingale passing through the rows of wounded and sick men at the barrack hospital at Scutari – the light from her little grecian urn illuminating the dreadful conditions into which she was bringing some semblance of order? Did I say the light from her little grecian urn? This is just one illustration of the necessity for intensive research before attempting to portray an historical character. Florence Nightingale was above all an entirely practical person and would not have dreamed of doing anything so inadequate as to carry a little grecian urn. But that was the way the artists and the writers of the period presented her to the public – that's how the legend has come down to us – as a symbol. When Herbert decided to film the life of Florence Nightingale my research began at the Imperial War Museum and almost the first exhibit I was shown was a Chinese lantern! It was the actual lamp carried by Miss Nightingale every night when she made her rounds at Scutari.

One lady who helped me enormously was Mrs Olive Prentice – for many years London director of the British Red Cross. Her mother, Mrs Bonham Carter, was Florence's favourite cousin and as girls they were inseparable. Mrs Prentice as a child often saw Florence and through her mother knew a great deal about her character. We spent some time at Claydon House, Buckinghamshire, where rooms originally designed by Chippendale were always at the disposal of Miss

Nightingale after her sister, Parthenope, married the widowed Sir Harry Verney in 1858. Sir Harry's grandson has told in a broadcast of knowing Florence Nightingale when he was a very small boy in the 1880's, of what fun she was and how she loved children. He painted a vivid, unexpected picture of her. Thanks to the co-operation of Dr King we were able to film at Embley Park in Hampshire, the residence of the Nightingales when they spent time in the south. Embley had become a boys' prep school but had retained a very distinct 'feel' of the Nightingale family. In the drawing room there is the marble mantelpiece by which Florence is standing with her pet owl, Athena. In this book is one of Parthenope's sketches of her. We met the owl, stuffed, in the Mayfair home of Mr Mitchelhill. It was still looking very wise. It is in a little churchyard close to Embley Park that Florence is buried – the simple headstone conveys nothing to the passing onlooker – just her initials, FN.

We were exceptionally fortunate to discover that Florence had spent much time at Broadlands, the beautiful home of the Mountbattens. Edwina Mountbatten – herself a modern Florence Nightingale – arranged for us to have unlimited facilities for filming at Broadlands. As a result of this co-operation Herbert put on a unique première of the film covering the whole of the Commonwealth (in those days a considerable Commonwealth) for the Royal College of Nursing, for which Lady Mountbatten was endeavouring to raise a large sum of money. These Commonwealth premières were highly successful and we have as a constant reminder the silver cigarette box given us by Lady Mountbatten and inscribed:

> 'To Herbert Wilcox and Anna Neagle
> with gratitude from nurses in all parts
> of the world and from all those devot-
> ed to the cause of nursing.
>
> September 22nd 1951.'

The London première at the Warner Theatre, Leicester Square, was probably without precedent and followed with drama. Their Royal Highnesses, Princess Elizabeth and Prince Philip had consented to attend and long before the scheduled time the square was packed. An urgent call came through from Buckingham Palace – it was Lord Mountbatten – their Royal Highnesses might not be there. Somehow this must have come through to the crowds waiting and it was a great tribute to their spirit that there were no moans or groans. They sensed something was wrong. It was; the King was very ill. Shortly, another call from Lord Mountbatten. 'We're on the way.' When the Royal party arrived at the theatre, instead of the usual cheering, the crowd were quiet. Once again they had sensed that all was not well. The Princess came up the stairs to meet the waiting members of the cast, looking radiant as you can see in the picture in this book. The film over, Herbert and I met the Royal party to see them away. Princess Elizabeth congratulated me and said, 'What a fighter she was.' We thanked her and I said that I hoped her news would be good. 'I hope so,' she answered. The next morning photographs of my meeting the Princess made the front pages of the dailies, but the headlines read:

'THE KING – AN OPERATION!'

Chapter Eighteen

ONE morning there was a ring on the door at Aldford House. A rather serious Michael Wilding came in and Herbert said, 'Hello,' and proceeded to get half a bottle of champagne from the refrigerator. He thought Michael looked as though he needed it. The cork popped.

'How are you, Michael?' asked Herbert.

'I've got a problem,' Michael replied.

'Drink up. Now what is it, Michael?'

'I want to marry Liz [Taylor],' he said.

'And she's turned you down?' Herbert asked.

'No, the idea seems to appeal to her – can't think why,' said Michael.

'Where's your problem?' Herbert asked.

'My contract with you,' was the unexpected reply.

'You see Liz is making films in Hollywood and if I'm making films in England, it would never work out.'

Herbert looked at me. 'Quite a problem – what do you think?'

'It's sad – but we must release him,' I answered. Michael came over and kissed me.

It was not long before the news made the front pages – world-wide. Herbert took Michael to the airport to meet Liz. These were incredible scenes at Heathrow, Herbert told me. From the VIP lounge he and Michael watched what looked like a 'demo'. Literally hundreds of journalists, photographers and a police escort surrounded the tiny figure of Elizabeth who was completely calm and master of the situation. In the airport when Michael greeted her with a kiss the photographers literally piled up on end to get their pictures.

Cameras were smashed – photographers trampled on. We'd asked the Registrar from Caxton Hall if he would kindly come to our flat so that a complete run-through of proceedings could be rehearsed. And I had suggested that I was sure Churchie, our wardrobe mistress and supervisor, would love to help Liz dress as she must have someone calm and efficient around her.

Herbert was to be best man – I was to be best girl.

The arrangements were that I would go to the Berkeley Hotel, where Elizabeth was to stay overnight, one hour before we were due at Caxton Hall.

Herbert was picking Michael up. The ceremony over we would return to Claridges where we had invited Michael's parents and some of Michael's and Liz's friends for a luncheon party.

Well, I arrived at the Berkeley as arranged – only to be told by the Hall Porter that Miss Taylor did not wish to be disturbed and he would take all messages. I explained the situation.

The Hall Porter phoned the room – line engaged. He then called the chambermaid who said the 'do not disturb' sign was still outside Miss Taylor's door. In desperation, I explained that I must go up to the room.

I knocked on the door. No answer. A second knock and as it opened I saw Churchie's anguished face – in her hand, a bunch of keys.

'Miss Taylor's still in bed,' she said, 'and there are six trunks and I don't know how many suitcases and I don't know *where* to look for the wedding dress. What am I to *do*, Miss Neagle?' She was nearly in tears.

This was Churchie, unflappable Churchie who always knew exactly where any item was to be found in her wardrobe department at the Studios with its hundreds of costumes and accessories.

I went into the bedroom. Liz was on the telephone; 'I'll never make it, Mike,' she was saying. She waved gaily to me, smiled that devastating smile, and went on talking. I looked at the stack of luggage. I understood Churchie's dilemma.

'Where's the dress?" I mouthed to Liz. She pointed to two trunks. 'Try the keys,' I whispered to Churchie. Luck was with us. There it was in the first she opened, an exquisite pearl grey dress designed for her by the head designer of the MGM Studios.

Liz took the quickest shower imaginable, Churchie laid out the dress and forty minutes later with a relaxed and radiant Liz, I left the hotel. We were only twenty minutes late!

I hope Churchie ordered herself a stiff drink but, knowing her, and having seen her surreptitiously 'water' the plants at Studio parties with a glass of alcohol, I am quite sure she didn't.

Chapter Nineteen

IT was now a good many years since I had played in the theatre and I missed the warm, immediate contact with audiences. With Coronation Year approaching, Tom Arnold, a great showman who had presented some of Ivor Novello's tremendous successes, discussed with Herbert an idea for a production with an historical and patriotic theme.

Robert Nesbitt produced and directed – the perfect choice for such a spectacular show written by Harold Purcell.

Choreography was in the hands of Philip and Betty Buchel. With the exception of *Piccadilly Incident*, for which brilliant Wendy Toye devised the dance sequences, the Buchels had choreographed the 'London Series'. Their dance for Michael and me in *Spring in Park Lane* was a highlight of the film.

As the play involved several periods in history, there were four leading men: Peter Graves, Patrick Holt, Olaf Olsen and James Carney. I was Nell Gwyn, Queen Victoria, a musical comedy star of the '14–18 and 1920s period, as well as a modern! I don't think I've ever enjoyed anything more.

We opened at Manchester for a six week season in the summer, and smashed every record. Then on to Glasgow, Coventry, Bristol and a Christmas season at Edinburgh. There was one scene, depicting an investiture, with the old Queen presenting the V.C. to a young soldier. This involved not only the full company but, in addition, a few 'supers' to 'dress' the scene as Guard Officers and Court Officials. In each city auditions were held to find the men who would fit into the picture – and the uniforms! Only sometime later did

I learn that one who appeared with us for the five weeks at Edinburgh was Sean Connery. This was his first job in show business.

We finally opened at the Palace Theatre, London, on a Saturday night in February 1953. The reaction of the audience grew increasingly enthusiastic as the evening progressed. It looked as though we were in for a huge success. Just towards the end of the show I was told not to take a curtain call so, quite as bewildered as the rest of the cast – and the audience – I found, the curtain just rose and fell and stayed down. Word had come round from the front that a group of actors in the gallery had resented the fact that the 'supers' engaged for the big scene were not all members of Equity (not obligatory at that time) and planned a demonstration. It was all such a great pity; the show was real entertainment. Tom Arnold and Emile Littler had arranged a big supper party at the Dorchester where, despite the phantom demo, everyone was happily enjoying the celebration. At our table was our old friend John Gordon of the *Sunday Express* who was quite lyrical about the show. Someone brought him a copy of his own paper, right off the presses. On the front page was a headline 'Anna Neagle Booed'. The article, by Logan Gourlay, described the booing which – if it happened at all, no one had heard – not even John Gordon himself. *The Glorious Days* wasn't a 'critics' show' but was very popular with audiences. However, with so many outside free attractions in connection with the Coronation, plus the fact that it was an enormously expensive production to maintain, we only ran through until November.

During the time we had been engaged on the gay 'London Series', Herbert and I had noticed a group of youngsters who were usually around if Michael and I were making an appearance anywhere. They were members of the Michael Wilding Fan Club. We grew to know them all, but there was one we especially liked – a shy girl with direct intelligent eyes. This was Joyce. Joyce even travelled to Manchester to cheer me on at that first night of *The Glorious Days*. She'd found there was a train from Euston at midnight getting into Manchester at 7 a.m. Perfect, she'd thought. What she hadn't discovered was that unless you booked a sleeper you were put off the train at 4 a.m.! Poor kid! I can't imagine how she kept her eyes open during that opening performance. But Joyce insists that she must have seen Manchester at its best, devoid of crowds and traffic, at dawn, on a beautiful July day.

During the London run she was often at the stage door and Herbert would chat with her whilst waiting for me. She looked like a school girl, but he discovered she was working in the publicity department of a film company in Wardour Street. She had collected a mine of information about our films and Herbert felt she would be of great value working in our publicity department. He asked if she would like to join us. And so Joyce came to our office in Mount Street. She was indeed a mine of information! She can still remember details of plots from our films which I've long forgotten. Later she was to tell me that she had first seen me when her father, on leave from the R.A.F., had taken her to see as a treat *The Wizard of Oz* and *Irene*, playing a double bill. From then on she'd seen most of our films. At that time, a weekly family visit to the local cinema was a 'must' and she recalls being sent ahead, as was the custom, to hold a place in the queue.

By 1960, she had become so much a part of our 'firm' that when my personal secretary, Carole Reid, left to get married. Joyce Wright took over her job at Aldford House. But she undertook far more than that. My aunt had been seriously ill the previous year, so Joyce stepped in to help look after her, and be around when I had to be away.

Early in the run of *The Glorious Days* a compliment was paid me which came as a great surprise – and honour; I was invited to be a member of The Executive Committee of The King George VI Memorial Foundation. The only other woman was Stella, Marchioness of Reading, known to all as the founder of the Women's Voluntary Services.

It had been decided that the monies donated by the British people should be used to benefit the elderly and the youth of the country. Lady Reading, with her expert knowledge, was invited to be Chairman of the Sub-Committee dealing specifically with the elderly. In discussions she was always to the point. Her suggestions for the best use to which the monies could be put and seeing the various projects carried through, were masterly.

The Committee consisted of a number of eminent men in many fields, but in my opinion none spoke or expressed his views with greater clarity than Lady Reading.

Meetings of the Committee were held over a period of seven years. Towards the end when the funds had been distributed the Chairman invited Lady Reading to report on her particular activities. She made a complete survey, always prefaced with '*my colleagues at* [say] Glasgow have now completed equipping the hostel, or *I am assured by my colleagues at* [say] Wolverhampton that the decorations will be completed in time for the Old People's Club' – etc., etc., and 'the special ramp for wheel chairs has been delivered.'

When she sat down there was a general murmur of agreement and approval, a question or two after which the Chairman turned to her saying, 'Is there anything else you would like to add, Lady Reading?'

'Yes,' she replied, disarmingly, 'I rather expected to take back to my colleagues, who have worked so hard, a vote of thanks from the Committee.'

A rare person indeed with her administrative ability, understanding and charm. How glad I am to have known her.

Herbert decided to make *The Glorious Days* into a film. Field Marshal Lord Montgomery, who had to see the play twice, bringing with him on the second occasion Lady Churchill, was most enthusiastic. They were both impressed by the patriotic flavour, the scope of the production and, sheer entertainment of the show. And as audiences consisted of large numbers of overseas visitors there was an indication it had a wide international appeal.

Another distinguished visitor to the Palace Theatre was the beautiful, extremely tall, Queen Salote of The Friendly Islands. I cannot imagine anyone more fitted to be Queen of The Friendly Islands – she was friendliness personified when she received me in the Royal Box. She told me she had been particularly interested in the investiture scene of Queen Victoria. 'You were very much as I have always imagined her,' she told me. 'I greatly admired her and have endeavoured to emulate some of her qualities: I hope I have succeeded.' I was reminded of Princess Juliana's comment regarding her mother, Queen Wilhelmina.

Queen Salote has become a legend. How she endeared herself to everyone on that Coronation day in 1953 when, despite torrential rain, an imposing colourful figure, she drove the entire length of the procession in an open carriage smiling and waving to all.

When the show closed, we took a short holiday in Sicily. In the train going back via Rome, Herbert noticed a paragraph in an Italian paper which said that Errol Flynn was in Rome. 'What about Errol for *Lilacs in the Spring*?' said Herbert. He'd chosen this title for the film of *Glorious Days*, as we were using Ivor Novello's lovely song as the theme music. 'As we're going to Rome,' Herbert went on, 'we could sound him out.' Herbert is never one to waste time!

And that we did. We found Errol a very engaging character, a fine actor and a marvellous-looking man, but there was something not quite right about our partnership. We didn't 'jell', at least not with the audiences who still, I believe, thought in terms of Michael-and-me. Also I think both Errol and I had big followings, but they were different people. Presumably those who wanted to see Errol didn't want to see me and vice-versa. Before we discovered this Herbert had signed him up for Ivor Novello's *King's Rhapsody*. He seemed the perfect choice for the role of the King of an imaginary Balkan country forced to abdicate leaving his beautiful young Queen (Patrice Wymore) and infant son to live in exile with his mistress.

King's Rhapsody was a headache from the beginning. Yugoslavia seemed an ideal country for location work and the idea was to make an Anglo-Yugoslav film. We found the people delightful, and very friendly, and the scenery just right. Then suddenly things began to go wrong. With the studio work in London completed, the Yugoslav Government decided against our filming in their country. We are still not sure of their reasons. Perhaps they felt that the story ran a little too close to their own history. The similarities were very slight, but they seemed so nervous about the whole thing that we decided there was nothing for it but to change horses in mid-stream.

After a great deal of searching we found our second 'horse' in Barcelona on the Mediterranean coast of Spain. I was glad it was Herbert, and not I, who had the problem of switching currencies – and that was only one of the difficulties. We needed mounted cavalry, and they do not exist in these days of mechanised warfare. Finally each separate hurdle was crossed and we went out to Barcelona where we were given permission to film in Franco's Palace. Then we went inland to the fantastic Montserrat mountain range, so well-known now to millions of English holiday-makers but very little known at the time. Wagner's *The Ring*, it is believed, was inspired by this extraordinary piece of country.

The last problem to overcome was one we had met before and hoped never to face again. Errol enjoyed his drink, more than a little. This made him unpredictable, sometimes almost impossibly so.

It was like working with Bob Newton again. But, what a fine actor he was – as was Bob when not enjoying their 'hobby'. No one, I think, could have played one or two of the very serious scenes, such as the Abdication in *King's Rhapsody*, better than he did.

It was Hugh Cudlipp, now Sir Hugh, the brilliant Editor of the *Daily Mirror*, who suggested over dinner one night that it was time I did a 'contemporary' film, if possible one with a problem theme which would find an echo in the minds and hearts of a large number of young-to-middle-age people. What about, say, 'The Generation Gap' – a phrase which was to become more and more familiar as the 'fifties progressed.

And so *My Teenage Daughter* was written for us by Felicity Douglas.

Sylvia Syms played the daughter who was to give me the sort of headaches and heartaches so many mothers were suffering at the time, and have suffered ever since.

Sylvia was only then on the threshold of her career, but she was absolutely right for the part, and played it beautifully. Kenneth Haigh, who created the part of Jimmy Porter in *Look Back in Anger*, and Wanda Ventham also got their first real breaks with this film.

Sylvia's younger sister was played by Margaret Lockwood's enchanting little daughter Julia, then eleven years old and, though a star's daughter, completely unspoiled.

Julia made an enormous impression on me right from the start. I marvelled that Margaret managed to bring her up so beautifully, whilst making such a fine career for herself at the same time. Margaret and I were often described as 'rivals' because we were both enjoying such great success at the same time. Dick Richards, in the *Sunday Pictorial*, once wrote that Margaret Lockwood and Anna Neagle stood out like Southend Pier! Alas, I hear the Pier may have to go – I hope we don't!

My Teenage Daughter was an outstanding success, and very timely. My rôle was that of a young war-widowed mother left to cope with a growing and rebellious girl. There must have been many hundreds like me in the country just then.

It made us realise that times were changing with a vengeance. We were now in the mid-fifties. The war was ten years behind us and many of the younger people had almost forgotten it. A new spirit was abroad, a great change was sweeping through the theatre and cinema, partly brought about by the advent of television. The films we had made for more than two decades for family entertainment, suddenly went out of fashion, just as 'Saturday night at the pictures' for the whole family went out of fashion. Now much of the family stayed at home and watched television instead. One could hardly blame them; once the set was bought or hired a whole week's entertainment was there for everyone, virtually free. And so the sort of entertainment we once provided, entered another medium and the theatre and cinema began to be taken over by the Realists, the Angry Young Men, Kitchen-sink Drama and, later still, by something a good deal less pleasant.

I still believe there will be a swing back; that people will again begin to want the more lighthearted, yet sincere, entertainment we tried to give them. Why else are 'old movies' so enormously popular on television?

It is not that I am against realism in entertainment; nothing could have been more real than *Odette*, and I saw merit in the posing of current problems, as I had myself in *My Teenage Daughter*. In fact the next film in which I became interested was another very real problem story: *These Dangerous Years*.

We first saw Frankie Vaughan taking part in a Charity Show. We were impressed by Frankie from the beginning. Apart from being a splendid artiste, he had great sincerity in his work, and his life. When I heard of his practical interest in the National Boys' Clubs this appealed to me strongly.

Everyone knows of course that members of the theatrical profession try to help charitable causes, undoubtedly influenced by the fact that we realise we have been fortunate not only in having interesting work but that the financial rewards to the really successful are so great. It was hearing about Frankie's interest in Boys' Clubs that, apart from his singing, drew us to him. One day I returned home to find Frankie having tea and a talk with Herbert. It appeared that he was doing very well as a singer on the Halls, and making records, but so far had done no acting, and he was very anxious to have an opportunity in films.

Through our conversation we learned something of his early background in Liverpool during the war, at the dangerous age between leaving school and being called up for the army. We decided that this would make an exciting and still topical theme for a film. The story was not, of course, Frankie's own, but since he had done no acting we felt that putting it in a familiar setting would help him.

As he talked about life near the Liverpool Docks my mind raced back to the time when I was taken by my mother to visit father's ship there. I recalled the neighbourhood clearly and could easily visualise the problems and difficulties of a youngster growing up during the nightly war-time blitz in such surroundings. Not long before I had read Jack Trevor Story's novel *The Trouble with Harry*, and it had stuck in my mind. We sent for Jack, and before we knew where we were we had the nucleus of an idea.

With Herbert to Produce and Direct . . . 'No,' said Herbert firmly. 'I will Direct, but this is your idea, so you will Produce.'

'Me!' I replied.

'Yes, you. You've always been interested in the technical side of film-making and co-produced with me. This time you are on your own.' Although I had co-produced several films with Herbert this time I became a solo Producer. And how different it was from acting! Always, before, when I had been making a film, I had been cushioned from outside disturbances; phone-calls were diverted, visitors gently ushered away. Not so now! People came to me from all sides, with masses of problems. The telephone never stopped ringing. The Casting Director came to talk about casting, down to the tiniest 'bit' part; the Art Director wanted me to agree plans for the sets (and how difficult it is, I found, to visualise the finished job from a paper-plan). The Production Manager contacted me constantly to keep me informed about daily details – location arrangements and so on.

Then there were costumes, and make-up, to discuss, press interviews and a hundred and one other things which I, with my long association with film work, had never given a thought to. And always always at the back of my mind was *money*. How much we could afford to spend on a film introducing a new idea and a new star, and how best to spend it. It gave me great insight into the intricacies of putting together a film, though I thought I knew most of them already.

To be honest I cannot say 'alone I did it'. Always at my shoulder were Herbert and his son John, our Production Manager, to help with advice or answer my questions. Without them I could never have carried it through especially in the early stages when everything was so bewildering.

But as the picture progressed I found myself taking more and more decisions on my own, and enjoying it. The fact that there are so few women producers leads many people to ask why I trespassed on what was obviously a man's preserve. I believe that there are ways in which a woman Producer can, in fact, be better than a man. At a script conference, for example, men often seem to have 'cardboard' ideas of what a girl is like, and what she is thinking. That's when a woman Producer can help, from her own understanding. I think, too, it can be a great help to the girls in the cast if one has been an actress oneself.

I had one or two apprehensive moments when we were shooting *These Dangerous Years*, especially when we went to shoot a rock'n'roll sequence in a famous dance-hall in North London. I was not quite sure what sort of reception we would get. As the film dealt with teenage boys and girls I wondered whether we would have any trouble from Teddy Boys who thought we were having a go at them. I couldn't have been more wrong. Instead of the bad behaviour I had been led to associate with the 'teds', I found nearly two thousand healthy youngsters enjoying themselves in a perfectly normal and good-mannered way.

When I left the hall I waited in the car for Herbert to join me. Soon a number of boys in the then-fashionable Edwardian clothing crowded round, and began tapping on the window. I admit that for a moment my heart fluttered. But I wound down the window and asked what they wanted.

'Excuse me, Anna,' one asked, 'but could you tell us how you get into this lark?' He thumbed over his shoulder at the extras who were just finishing a shot. I tried to explain the rules for entering the film industry, warned them of the difficulties involved, and the set-up of the Film Artistes' Association. The 'teds' listened quietly until I had finished. 'Thanks a lot – Anna,' they said and went away.

These Dangerous Years was a great success. Frankie had a huge following as a cabaret and record artiste and was awarded the Variety Club Award as the outstanding newcomer to British films. Later I produced two more films with him, but meanwhile I was glad to get back on to my own side of the fence.

Herbert was finishing-off directing the last scenes of *These Dangerous Years*, and so for the first and last time in my career I had a different Director, Cyril Frankel, for *No Time for Tears*, in which I played the part of a hospital Matron, with Flora Robson, Sylvia Syms and Angela Baddeley, now so popular on television as the cook in *Upstairs, Downstairs*. Adrienne Posta played a child in the hospital, and was delightful.

Once again I found great help from people outside the profession, especially from the Matrons of the Great Ormond Street Hospital and Victoria Children's Hospital, Chelsea.

Frankie fulfilled all our hopes as an actor and we would have liked to put him under contract again but once his name began to be known in the film world Hollywood offers began to come too, and he succumbed, as did Jackie Lane who played in two films with him.

Herbert and I thought neither of them quite ready for Hollywood ,though naturally we didn't stand in Frankie's way, the more so because he was cast to play with Marilyn Monroe, a wonderful opportunity for him. As we feared, Hollywood didn't 'take' with either one of them. We lost track of Jackie and Frankie came home and went back to his true love, Cabaret and Variety, where he has continued, happily, to bring in the audiences despite the ever-changing styles of music.

For the last few years my work in the theatre has brought me into close contact with young people. I must admit I don't quite get the appeal of 'pop', although the rythyms fascinate me and some of the lyrics reflect an awareness of other people's problems. But the frankness of the younger generation! Their expertise at the job in theatre and studio! Their ability to fend for themselves – especially the girls, with all their shopping and cooking – some even looking after husbands and children. It never ceases to amaze me. If I wore a hat these days I'd certainly take it off to them.

Chapter Twenty

NOT very long ago I was one of the 'guests' on *This Is Your Life*. The 'subject', clever John Alderton, who had been with me in *Person Unknown*. I was asked by so many people, as I had been on a number of similar occasions, 'They aren't really taken by surprise, are they? They must know it is going to happen.' I assure them that when I was the 'victim' it came as a complete shock. It happened at the end of *These Dangerous Years*. Stanley Black was composing the background music for the picture and it was thought that my discussing this with him would make an interesting item on a TV programme the BBC were running at the time. I duly arrived at the studio, the old Shepherd's Bush Empire. After being made up, I was called down for a rehearsal. Stanley was already at work with the orchestra, set up under the Circle. We worked for a few minutes on a certain passage of music to go under a scene, then started a run through.

Almost immediately the lights dimmed. I looked around to see what was amiss, to find Eamonn Andrews, with that engaging crooked smile of his, holding out a hand to me and saying: 'Anna Neagle, This Is Your Life!'

He led me up to the stage in a complete daze.

As he talked to me, photographs of my early days in the theatre were thrown on the TV screen we were watching and then followed a scene of Jack Buchanan and me in *Goodnight Vienna*. Only a few weeks before Jack had died and seeing him there made me very emotional. I hadn't time to pull myself together before the guests were coming on, all saying the kindest things. I always am far more upset by kindness than harshness. Perhaps this is a strange contradiction but this is how it affects me. I was very weepy. The next day, one paper had a headline 'This key-hole snooping should stop'. Well meant, I'm sure, but when thinking about the whole experience later on, realised the compliment we are paid by Eamonn and his colleagues who invite us on the programme.

I also realised that I'd been extremely slow-witted. Maybe two or three weeks before there had been a telephone call from Miss Archibald (my former Headmistress) who, after a few moments chat, had asked if Herbert was in. I called him to the phone, then went off to do something. I am not by nature curious, apart from things that concern me, so didn't even ask him what she had to say. I'm sure I supposed she was wondering if he could suggest someone to open a bazaar or fête, as I had done for her the previous year.

Need I add, Miss Archibald was one of the guests on my *This Is Your Life*!!

It was around this time that audience taste began to change so dramatically. The considerable profits made by our run of tremendous successes, especially the 'London Series' and *Odette*, together with the entire amount due to us was invested in British Lion shares. Unfortunately some other productions for the company were losing more than ours had made. The result was that soon the Government decided to wind British Lion up, and our entire savings went up in smoke.

Chapter Twenty-one

BOTH Herbert and I were admirers of Rose Heilbron, Q.C., who was making legal history in Lancashire. He got an idea that for me to play a modern Portia would be the right subject for my next film.

Edgar Lustgarten was commissioned to write a script. Anthony Quayle was fixed as leading man and Zsa Zsa Gabor was the victim of a murder.

For some reason the combination of Zsa Zsa and myself met with a sceptical reaction, but we ignored it. I found her a first-class actress, very beautiful and extremely witty.

It made, for me, a quite fascinating picture, *The Man who Wouldn't Talk*. As so often it was the research beforehand which I enjoyed as much as the filming. Edgar Lustgarten introduced us to Edgar Bowker, for thirty-five years Clerk and Administrator of the Chambers for those 'greats' of the Court, Marshall Hall, with whom he served for fifteen years, and Norman Birkett, with whom he worked for twenty years. (He had also been judges clerk at the Nuremberg trials.) 'Clerk' is a misleading word for this type of important, responsible work. Edgar Bowker was as knowledgeable about the Law, and the Courts, as anybody one is likely to meet.

I had myself served on a jury in St Albans in 1938 and so had a little personal experience, but I learned a great deal more from Mr Bowker. He took me to the Old Bailey opening session where I watched the ritual of Sheriffs and the Lord Mayor, with their traditional nosegays of flowers and herbs, dating back to the time when Courts of Law were less

Top left: The première of *Odette*. HM the Queen, Odette, and myself.
Top right: As Florence Nightingale at her home, Lea Hurst, Derbyshire, showing the balcony from which she spoke to the villagers on her return from the Crimea.
Bottom: The royal première of *The Lady with a Lamp*, attended by HRH the Princess Elizabeth and the Countess Mountbatten. With me are Herbert, Michael Wilding, Gladys Young and Anthony Collins.
Previous page: As Odette at Ravensbrück Concentration Camp.

17 May 1953

Dear Miss Neagle

I would like to say how very
much I enjoyed "the Glorious Days"
last night.

To: Anna Neagle

the supreme actress of modern times.
From a soldier admirer.

Montgomery of Alamein
F.M.

June 1953

Previous page: Field Marshal Montgomery of Alamein, K.G.
Top: In a dance sequence from *Lilacs in the Spring*, the film version of *The Glorious Days*.
Centre: An unusual picture of Errol Flynn when he danced with me in *Lilacs in the Spring*.
Bottom left: Addressing the congregation at Norwich Cathedral on the fiftieth anniversary of the execution of Nurse Edith Cavell, who is buried in the precincts.
Bottom right: With Edward Bowker, clerk to Sir Marshall Hall and Lord Birkett, who acted as adviser for *The Man Who Wouldn't Talk*. On my right is Anthony Quayle.

Top: A scene from *My Teenage Daughter* in which Sylvia Syms made her film début.
Centre: Finale of the record-breaking *Charlie Girl*. *(From left)* Derek Nimmo, Hy Hazell, Christine Holmes and Joe Brown. *(Photograph by Tom Hustler).*
Bottom: My two marvellous dancing partners in *Charlie Girl*. Roy Allan *(left)* and David Toguri. *(Photograph by Tom Hustler).*

Top: With Herbert outside Buckingham Palace after my investiture with the D.B.E., July 22nd 1969.

Centre: Guests of the Duke of Windsor aboard the SS *Queen Elizabeth* with Cecil Beaton, Herbert and Clifton Webb.

Bottom right: My beloved Tuppence.

Bottom left: Christmas, 1971 with Johnny Farnham and Derek Nimmo in *Charlie Girl*, Melbourne.

Top: The big tap routine in *No, No, Nanette* at the Theatre Royal, Drury Lane, 1973 (*Copyright Zoe Dominic*).
Centre: Rehearsing *I Want to be Happy*, for *No, No, Nanette*.
After-rehearsal discussion with Donald Sadler, the U.S. choreographer, and his assistant Bobby Becker (both kneeling foreground). (*Both pictures: copyright the Daily Express*).

Top : HM Queen Elizabeth the Queen Mother congratulating Herbert and myself following the gala performance of *Sixty Glorious Years* at the Odeon, Leicester Square, 1973. HM King George VI at the première of *Odette* at the Plaza Theatre, June 6th, 1950.

sweet-smelling than they are today! There I sat through a muder trial, amongst other things. Mr Bowker also arranged for me to visit Lewes Assizes and afterwards I had tea with the two Judges, who kindly exchanged anecdotes about different cases, purely for my benefit.

Anthony Quayle played my client, in a complicated story involving Secret Intelligence. It was a very tense situation since he was accused of murder and this was before Capital Punishment was abolished.

It was during this film that I tackled one of the most difficult film sequences of my career. I had one very long closing speech, lasting for six minutes, which is a lot of film! It was decided to do this in one uninterrupted shot, starting with the camera in the distance, gradually closing in on to my face. It was, I was told at the time, the longest uncut shot on record. Luckily I made it in one. I don't think I could have tackled it a second time! For the theatre there would be nothing remarkable about this because there would have been several weeks for rehearsal which, of course, doesn't apply when filming. The crowded 'court' with more than a hundred actors applauded me. Something I had never known before. Herbert showed the film to the press in New York and at the end of this, the longest take without a cut they had ever seen, they, too, applauded. Kate Cameron on the New York *Daily News* told Herbert, 'It's a masterpiece, Anna's greatest perfomance.'

For London Herbert had arranged a special showing for the legal profession in the Law Courts but with the discord at British Lion our Law Courts première was abandoned. Shortly afterwards a première *did* take place there of Hitchcock's film *Witness for the Prosecution*, which spectacular launching undoubtedly helped its subsequent phenomenal success.

That upheaval at British Lion was the first cloud on our hitherto almost cloud-free horizon. It was the sign of the storm to come. If we had been spoiled so far by success we were about to see the other side of the picture. If at one time we could do nothing wrong, now, it seemed, we could do nothing right! *The Lady is a Square* was, I thought, an ideal film with something for everyone; it was a gay picture blending the two different types of music perfectly. It went out in the summer of 1959; a summer when it seemed the sun never stopped shining. And who wanted to go to the pictures while the sun shone in England? It was a disastrous season not only for us, but for cinemas and theatres all over the country.

I was very disappointed by this, but at that time still shattered by the sudden death of my brother Stuart the previous Christmas, and haunted by the sad beauty of his Memorial Service at St Paul's Cathedral.

A projected television series about Ann Brusselmans, who had so heroically hidden and helped a great many R.A.F. escapees in Belgium during the war, died before it reached the little screen.

It was as though some malevolent demon had been waiting in the wings for us for years, and brought out his entire bag of tricks at the same moment.

Herbert and his city associates paid £100,000 to Terence Rattigan for the film rights of his play *Ross*, only to find that another film about Lawrence of Arabia was challenging his rights. On legal advice he dropped it and the money was lost.

He made a wonderful film version of *The Beggar's Opera* with Sir Laurence Olivier which proved to be almost total disaster. It was nobody's fault, certainly not the star's or producer's. Quite simply, it was made before its time.

Yangtse Incident, Herbert's magnificent film about the escape of H.M.S. *Amethyst* from a mud-bank in the Yangtse river, under shell-fire from the Communists, appeared after, not before, another great naval picture *The Battle of the River Plate* which scooped the pool.

When British Lion finally crashed, it took with it almost all we had made over the years of plenty.

Herbert was magnificent. He did everything possible to hide from me the seriousness of our financial situation. I knew he was worried – so was I – but he used all kinds of subterfuges to cover up. Much later he told me that every morning when he made our morning tea he sifted through the post and extracted the mounting bills before I could see them. He went out each day with his briefcase, and a cheery smile, searching for a solution. Then he had a brainwave.

Remembering the joy I had had from dancing in my early days, and knowing how successful the Fred Astaire Dancing Schools were in America, he thought the combination of Fred Astaire and myself could not fail. He applied for, and received, permission for me to start a similar organisation in England.

I have always made it a strict rule not to lend my name to anything in which I do not feel wholeheartedly in sympathy and agreement. Shortly before I'd had an offer of a very big fee for a TV commercial. The sponsors assured me that the product was impeccable and indeed I know of the high regard felt for the firm producing it. 'After all,' they told me, 'the biggest names in the country realise that this is a new medium and . . .' I hesitated but finally decided that I didn't want to depart from my principle. (Ironically, another actress accepted, and made the commercial which was never shown, having after much deliberation been turned down by the Authority!)

With the proposed dancing school I knew that here was something with which I was completely in sympathy. Not only would it give enjoyment to people of all ages, but it would also give lonely ones a chance of meeting people and gaining the confidence, as well as fitness which comes from the perfect exercise of dancing. It must, I decided, be done well. My Board of Directors carried an impressive list of famous names, amongst them my very great friend Odette.

Premises were found in Old Bond Street, a new building in which was created a beautiful dancing school. Sprung floors were laid in the two main studios. There were rooms for private tuition; there were staff quarters, office accommodation and reception area. All of which cost a great deal of money, but this time I was confident of success.

I took on a staff of sixteen: excellent instructors, a Manageress, Manager, Secretary. I put them all on salary because I felt that working on commission might tempt them to 'push' people into taking lessons, and I didn't want that. I applied for Fire Permits, permission to use the premises for Music and Dancing – almost for permission to *breathe*! I don't think I have ever worked harder in my life.

We hoped to open in the autumn of 1961, but we were not ready. We opened instead in the spring of 1962, literally with a bang: Humphrey Lyttleton and his orchestra in one ballroom, Tommy Kinsey and his orchestra in the other, so that there were two styles of music. We provided a fantastic buffet and invited lots of people to become Founder Members at advantageous rates. Everyone agreed that we were on a real winner. We were not. We hit *just* the wrong moment. Non-dancing, as I feel it to be, was succeeding. The twist was sweeping the States and was soon to sweep this country. Television's *Come Dancing* had yet to become the nation-wide presentation which brought about the great revival of my style of ballroom dancing. My private demon just made sure that I fell between two stools and took a lot more money with me – not by any means all of it mine. The only good thing to emerge was that our school introduced the Bosa

Nova to England! Peter Sellers, needing to know something about the new dance for a sequence in *The Pink Panther*, the picture he was making then, came along to the school. So clever is he and so instinctive his rhythm, within an hour or two he was as expert as our expert instructor! Could the school have carried on through that winter, we might have survived, but it was too big a risk to take. Reluctantly my Board decided we must close and put the company into voluntary liquidation.

Two television plays for our old friend, John Woolf, head of Anglia TV, just about kept our heads above water.

Towards the end of the year a script was sent me inviting me, if interested, to make a six-week tour. Just that, no more. It wasn't the type of play I'd done before but I accepted. *Person Unknown* proved to be not only a financial help but a great morale booster. The company presenting it, and the cast, were a great 'team', keen, enthusiastic and professional. Of course it hadn't brought in enough for us to solve our major problems and ultimately we had to dispose of many of our 'treasures': the pictures, jewellery, the Epstein bust, our lease of Aldford House and the furniture – really almost everything. I think I most regretted the Bechstein piano going. It was the first important thing I'd ever bought and I loved it.

It was all rather like living in a nightmare. We had our small Brighton flat and a trickle of royalties from old films.

My aunt, now eighty-seven, was at the Brighton flat, which became our 'base'. Auntie's spirit remained indomitable but she was becoming increasingly infirm. It was a constant anxiety finding someone to be with her. A succession of kindly friends and part-time helps rallied round. Mrs Baker who had always looked after the Brighton flat for us was a tower of strength, although she had her own family to look after. Inevitably there were gaps in the time-table. These were mainly filled by Joyce, who took an enormous load off our shoulders.

Soon after Christmas, it having been decided to send out another tour of *Person Unknown*, I was in the midst of rehearsing for the opening at Golders Green, the following Monday, when Herbert met me at the rehearsal room, and took me to a nearby pub for a drink. He told me that Auntie had died, quite suddenly, that morning. I remembered her final good-bye when I left the flat after the previous weekend. 'Well, I expect I'll see you when I see you then.' Well, she wouldn't any more. Someone who had been a part of my life, *all* my life, had gone. Unselfishly she had dedicated herself to my family and for so many years to me in particular.

Joyce had been alone with her those last few days and the strain and shock were considerable. Also, no doubt, she had guessed more about our problems than we realised. Now she was to discover an overwhelming one of her own.

Her mother had several times told me she was worried about Joyce. She looked so far from well. We persuaded her to see her doctor who arranged for her to have a thorough check up. The findings were almost unbelievable. Although she had never been very robust, no one had discovered, through all her growing-up years, that she had lived all her life with a hole in her heart! As soon as it was possible to arrange it, she went into St George's Hospital for a difficult and delicate operation. It was entirely successful.

In an endeavour to keep the ship afloat Herbert had been borrowing from private sources at high interest rates. In 1964 the axe fell. As I have indicated, it left us with few material possessions. Even the Awards given to Herbert went (although they are now happily restored to us). I say deliberately that we were stripped of our *material* possessions because if there is one thing disaster does, it sorts out your priorities, and it sorts out your real friends from those who merely want to share your success.

We had no idea how many true friends we had. Some we knew intimately, some we had never met. One close friend offered us her country cottage as a temporary home. Vivien Leigh and Laurence Olivier tried hard to make us take back a small but valuable Corot Herbert had given him when making *The Beggar's Opera*. Of course we refused, but other offers we could not refuse; small gifts from well-wishers who would have been hurt by a rebuff.

I treasure a letter signed merely 'A Brummie family', sending 'a small contribution' as a thank-you for all the pleasure we had given them over the years. Herbert still carries a note from the Matron of a home for the elderly, which enclosed a five pound note, the result of a whip-round.

What could one do? Where the letters were signed I at first wrote back asking permission to return the money, or give it to charity, but invariably received hurt replies. The writers, like my Brummie family, wanted only to help *us*, and for the same reason.

Another thing we had not lost, apart from our friends, was the will to overcome our troubles. I have never admired Herbert more than I did at that time. Most men, after a lifetime's endeavour and so much success, might have given up, turned bitter or felt unable to fight back. But he was still bursting with ideas.

The one bright spot in all this gloom was meeting Tuppence. Following a few months' tour, which was highly successful and extremely interesting since it took me to towns I'd never played in before, I was able to meet and stay with old friends I'd had little opportunity of seeing previously. I returned to Brighton. There were many things needing my attention as I'd not been able to go down since my aunt's death. Joyce, now recovered from her very serious operation, came with me and then – Tuppence arrived in our lives, a small, determined, beautiful ball of fur and fire. Large golden eyes that could turn to dark thunder of sudden anger, completed the picture. She was 'all cat' and wouldn't have thanked me for describing her as almost human. She wasn't everyone's cat either. She liked, or disliked – and it worked in reverse.

She adopted us at Brighton and it was weeks before we discovered she had a perfectly good home of her own. The only problem seemed to be her son, Whitesocks, who, according to Tuppence's code should have left the nest. Timid and chaste, the exact opposite to his mother, he hadn't. We discovered she made a habit of returning home about once a week to partake of a good dinner, provoke Whitesocks to a round of fisticuffs which always ended in disaster since Whitesocks was far too gentle a cat to be provoked by anyone – far less his mother who had a lethal left hook. Eventually after mutual agreement with her owner it was decided she was to live permanently with us.

All cat though she was, she didn't conform in every way to her species. A farm cat by birth she hunted as was her nature, but we never saw her 'play' or torture her prey. Birds didn't appear to interest her. Mice and rats from the garden were killed outright with a single blow. Once dead, they were left, or if the fancy took her, presented to the person of her choice. The only difficulty, then, was to dispose of the corpse without hurting her feelings.

That summer I was asked to take part in a big charity show *Night of a Hundred Stars* at the London Palladium. The producers thought it would be amusing if I did a gay number with ten famous young actors and singers. Actually we combined two. The boys were in bathing costumes of around 1910 and I was a bathing belle of the period. The boys sang to me *Does your mother know you're out, Cecilia?* and I sang back to them a number recently revived by Dorothy Provine

I Don't Care. It was all enormous fun and the result completely unexpected. In the audience were two young men, John Taylor, the composer, and Ross Taylor, who together had plans for a musical play. The next morning their agent was in touch. We asked for the script. Herbert read it first and passed it on to me. 'Any good?' I asked anxiously, knowing how badly we needed the money.

'If nothing else,' replied Herbert, 'you'd be well cast. A Cochran Young Lady who marries into the aristocracy. Her husband dies – she inherits a stately home – but no money!'

I read it, and saw the enormous popular potential. Harold Fielding was presenting the show and my co-star was Joe Brown. There was a lot of preparation to be done by the producers, so I went off on yet another tour of *Person Unknown*. By the time I got back, all was set up – David Heneker, Hugh and Margaret Williams, together with Ray Cooney.

There was one of my numbers which especially appealed to me but I'd not done any singing or dancing for quite some time, so needed to put in time studying. Kenneth Alwyn, the Musical Director, introduced me to Harold Miller, who had trained or coached so many fine artistes in all types of singing. His pupils included opera singers and pop stars. Once rehearsals of *Charlie Girl* began I was at his studio at 9.30 a.m. before dashing on to the Adelphi for a short time with Kenneth Alwyn and then into the main work of the day. I'll never fail to appreciate this help from two such busy people. Wallace Douglas was directing the play with Alfred Rodriguez, who also choreographed. There was a delightful dance routine for me with David Toguri. I adored dancing again and with David it was a joy. There was the dancing of a charleston and jitterbug with Hy Hazell, also playing a former Cochran Young Lady. Hy was a great performer and a great person. Her untimely death was indeed a shock. The entire cast was splendid. Anyone who saw the show knows what an impact Derek Nimmo made with his unique reading of what could have been quite a stereotyped rôle.

The try-out at Golders Green was almost postponed, owing to problems of a set which caused an accident to the designer. It seemed we just wouldn't be able to open at all. Actually the show did go on – two days late and from the first performance audiences loved it. The strain of the financial blizzard we had recently weathered and the near miss with *Charlie Girl*, which might have meant such a bad opening that the show couldn't have survived, had been pretty overwhelming. There were changes and improvements to be rehearsed throughout the ten days at Golders Green. Herbert never left me, trying to lighten the load for me in any way he could. On the morning of our last two performances there, I was due for rehearsal, Herbert looked so ill I asked him not to come that day and he agreed to miss the matinee but would be with me in the evening. Joyce came during the afternoon and later told me that Herbert wouldn't be down after all. When I got back he was obviously very ill. He'd called his doctor who had diagnosed congestion. That night he sat in his chair. By 6 a.m. on Sunday morning he asked me to ring the doctor. At 8.30 a.m. he was in hospital having suffered a thrombosis, which I didn't know at the time. When I'd seen him settled in the care of the nurses, I went back to the mews cottage we'd rented to get ready for the recording session for *Charlie Girl*. With that over I went in to see Herbert. He looked much better but was in an oxygen tent. I was relieved to know he was in the right hands. *Charlie Girl* opened a few days later, on December 15th 1965, at the Adelphi Theatre. This was to be the first time Herbert hadn't been beside me for an opening or film première. I phoned just before the curtain went up. Sister told me he was asleep.

During the evening Joyce phoned Herbert with the connivance of Fred, the Stage-door keeper. Herbert had managed to get a telephone in the oxygen tent! He'd been given progress reports! The audience reaction was quite overwhelming but I couldn't wait to get to the hospital to report to Herbert. Although after midnight, Matron had given permission for me to go to his room and have a glass of champagne.

Despite the indifferent reviews, *Charlie Girl* was to run more than five years at the Adelphi. Record after record was broken. Harold Fielding did a great job of showmanship.

Meanwhile, despite a thrombosis, Herbert was now back to full health, his discharge from bankruptcy well and truly behind us and the world once again was a good place to live in.

In the early days of *Charlie Girl* Tuppence was cared for during the week by friends in the neighbouring flat. However, we found it hard to leave the small face that somehow always managed to be watching from the window as we left. Our arrival home each weekend was always greeted by an extremely sleepy, but happy cat. A short purr of welcome and she was back to bed. Tuppence had very strong views about bed. If we came home at all hours, that was our affair, but five minutes later, safe in the knowledge we were back, she would be flat out, in a dreamland all of her own. Inevitably, we gave way to the face at the window. Tuppence came to London. Herbert was in New York on a business trip and since neither Joyce nor I, for that matter, wished to look complete fools, and since we didn't know what his reaction to having a 'London' cat would be, we chose that time to load her into the car, complete with sleeping basket, cat litter, collar, lead and food. It was then only necessary to cross our fingers and trust that she was the cat we thought she was. Intelligent and adaptable. She didn't disappoint us – ever. She didn't, of course, sleep in the basket. Regarded the cat litter as ours, for *our* use, and dug up the nearest neighbouring rose-beds. The collar and lead she would have donated happily to women's lib! She certainly never wore it unless we were under extreme provocation. Herbert's arrival was awaited with bated breath. He greeted her – with delight! Seeing Tuppence, he said, made it really feel like home.

When we gave up the Brighton flat, Tuppence actually *chose* our new home! We went to view. Naturally she came too. The garden boasts the most beautiful Hydrangea bush. She sat in the middle flatly refusing to come out and using every tooth, claw and some quite unprintable language to that end. It was either buy the lease – or the bush!

She loved, hated, played, was outrageously rude and completely vulnerable to a harsh word. She fawned to no-one – dined at the Savoy, picnicked on Wimbledon Common and, of course, came to the theatre. I shall always remember her running down the stairs of the Adelphi Theatre to my dressing room – she was always first. She saw the suitcases – which meant 'going away'. We took to packing surreptitiously, but were always found out. It is decidedly uncomfortable – as every animal-lover will understand – to pack a suitcase while accusing eyes watch every move. She came to airports oblivious of the noise around her, quite calm, to see us off. She flirted outrageously with the Personnel – she seemed to understand that if airports meant going away they also meant she would be brought to the same place when we came back. Another 'dislike' were phoney 'cat lovers' – which species of humanity she could spot a hundred yards off. She was, in fact, the only cat I ever knew who didn't try to win a non-cat lover over to her side.

On June 14th 1969 I woke up to hear on the radio and read in the papers that I had been created a Dame of the British Empire. I had been notified of course that it was proposed to put my name forward but this doesn't necessarily mean the honour will be conferred. I cannot recall when I've had so exciting a day (telephone never stopped ringing, a string of telegrams) or night. It was Saturday night when the Adelphi was always packed, and this night even standing room was not available. My dressing-room was literally packed with flowers and the cast all came to my dressing-room to congratulate me. At the end of the performance I used to walk down the baronial hall staircase to the tune of my big number *I was young*. But not tonight! Derek Nimmo had other ideas, and quickly passed word to the entire cast and orchestra.

As I commenced to descend the stairs, the orchestra started up and the entire cast sang *There's Nothing like a Dame*. And then the audience took it up. I was too choked with emotion to say much. Herbert, too, regarded this as the most moving moment he has experienced.

The show over, my dressing-room was 'open house' with drinks, laid on by Herbert.

How often have I heard about the petty jealousies of the acting profession? Every face reflected pleasure and happiness. We went on until the small hours and throughout it all Tuppence perched herself in the best chair and had the longest and greatest petting of her life. A gloriously happy occasion.

When *Charlie Girl* finished at the Adelphi, it had been seen by 1,500,000 people and had taken £2,400,000 at the box office. A short holiday followed – then a tour of Australia and New Zealand was arranged. With 2,047 performances I personally established an all-time record for any star artiste in the West End. A record commemorated by a luncheon at the Garrick Club in my honour.

Before leaving this, I would like to tell you briefly of my investiture. Everyone is, of course, well briefed and proceedings are invariably standard. When I approached the Queen, her fact lit up as she said to me: 'I'm very happy to give you this. You work so very hard.' That coming from the Queen – probably the hardest worked woman in the country touched me very much.

Chapter Twenty-two

IN August 1971 we took off. We were opening at Melbourne.
The cast was mainly Australian. Johnny Farnham, originally
from England, but now a real young Australian, and their
top pop singer and recording star for the past five years, was
a splendid 'Joe'. Roy Allen, the marvellous Jamaican dancer
who had taken over from David Toguri as my dancing partner
in London, came with us and, of course, Derek repeated his
success. Freddie Carpenter re-produced the show.

The five big cities of Australia was the target but we never
got beyond Melbourne, where, for eight months the business
was even bigger than at the Adelphi. The drive and enthusiasm
reminded me of Hollywood when I first worked there. I
experienced so much kindness, too, in and out of the theatre.

One most interesting visit was to the country home of
Dame Nellie Melba, where my brother Stuart had stayed
when making the tour with Melba back in 1927. I was taken
there by Melba's daughter-in-law and grand-daughter.
The house has retained so much of the atmosphere Dame
Nellie had created. It was thrilling to hear some of her records played on an old gramaphone in that setting – of course
they were rough and 'tinny' but the high notes soared through
with such beauty. How I wished I'd heard her sing in person.

Another memorable visit was to the R.A.A.F. Headquarters,
Point Cook. The C.O. 'Air Commodore Col. Quohoun' invited me to attend the Armistice Service, a very moving
experience indeed, as was the Edith Cavell Memorial Service
at Melbourne.

Before leaving London, Herbert and I had been invited by the Lord Mayor and Lady Mayoress of Melbourne, Mr and Mrs Edward Best, to attend a big function at the end of their term of office. So upon arrival in the City we were immediately made to feel 'at home' and given such a warm welcome. Mrs Best was to prove a tower of strength when Herbert arranged a special Gala Performance of *Sixty Glorious Years* shortly before we left Australia – the like of which Melbourne had never seen before, they told us.

We had two visits to Sydney – the first a sad one. Herbert had not seen his brother Joe for many years so, the first weekend we'd flown up, knowing he was very ill. I'd never met Joe and his wife and I was very glad to be able to do so then. Joe, a great character, died a few days later.

The second visit, before leaving for New Zealand, was to meet my cousins – on the Neagle side – Michael Terry I'd not met since he had come to England in 1924 to be made a Fellow of the Royal Geographical Society. He and a friend had carried out an extraordinary job of exploration in making the first crossing of the Northern Territory in a Ford car when there were no roads of any description. Having seen just a little of the undeveloped part of Australia as it is, even today, the journey was an incredible achievement.

At Auckland we were to repeat the fantastic success of Melbourne. The audiences just loved *Charlie Girl*. But once again, the planned tour of both the North and South Islands had to be abandoned. We stayed on at Auckland for the whole period.

The Charity Gala Performance of *Sixty Glorious Years* was repeated there and it is very interesting, I think, that the film played at both Auckland and Melbourne for eight weeks against the so-called 'permissive society' films which had been swamping the cinemas. After thirty-five years, it was again hailed as a great picture.

After six and a half years of *Charlie Girl*, I was very tired and Herbert also was feeling the strain, no doubt heightened by his having to make three round trips to London in connection with the Gala performances of *Sixty Glorious Years*.

Once again, warmth and friendliness from the people of New Zealand, some of whom had met my father when he had visited their parents during his days as a Captain in the New Zealand Shipping Company.

We were guests of the Commodore of the company aboard one of their ships. A most nostalgic day for me. Another Commodore of the company who had made his first voyage as a cadet with my father told me how grateful he'd always felt that he had such a first 'Old Man' – Father must have been all of forty-eight! But, as I expect many of my readers will know, that is a good old seafaring term.

Then there was Don Lochore of the New Zealand *Herald*, whom Herbert and I put in the same critical class as Caroline Lejeune and Kate Cameron, displaying both heart and intellect. As a young reporter Don had interviewed my father on that last trip he'd made and remembered him vividly.

From the moment Don got to know Herbert and me we became friends and it was such a pleasure to us that he and his charming wife could be present at the Commonwealth Observance Day Service at Westminster Abbey in 1973 when I had been invited to read a poem to the congregation which included H.M. The Queen and Prince Philip. Prayers were spoken by representatives of every country. A most impressive occasion.

One other pleasant memory of Auckland I shall never forget was my visit to Selwyn City. This wonderful experiment is one that I wish could be copied throughout the world.

Selwyn City is the brainchild of Sir Robert Kerridge. He realised that the enemy of old age pensioners (senior citizens) is not only lack of money but loneliness. In Selwyn City, they have companionship in plenty, their own church, shopping centre, cinema, and rooms or bungalows for one or two – altogether a wonderful conception. There is no loss of freedom or dignity. The people looked so contented.

I know we have something of this nature but, on a small scale, in the Abbeyfield Houses. The complete community-conception of Selwyn City must make it a unique experiment.

The South Island had expected *Charlie Girl* to play there and a fabulous offer also came from Sydney.

Reluctantly I had to decline as I felt it unwise to go. I told Herbert I felt rather ill, something he had rarely heard me say. I just felt I couldn't go on beyond our present commitments. He agreed with me so, after six years and four months of quite one of my happiest professional experiences, I said good-bye to *Charlie Girl* and good-bye to New Zealand.

I wanted to do nothing now but sleep – to feel well again.

I was sorry to miss Wellington and Christchurch and the other cities I'd hoped to visit. I was sorry to disappoint Sydney, but I felt completely drained and could not get home soon enough to rest for a while.

I felt more myself when we reached Heathrow. Joyce was there but not my darling Tuppence. She'd been rather unwell and Joyce thought if there was any delay in our arrival, even Tuppence, the perfect Airport Cat, might get restless.

Once home I went to bed to recover from the exhausting flight. A few good nights' sleep, home cooking and the garden would soon put me right I thought, and hoped.

But it didn't.

Chapter Twenty-three

BEFORE leaving New Zealand I'd had word that Binkie (Hugh) Beaumont would like to meet me when I arrived back in London. Ever since the wartime tour of *French Without Tears* I'd hoped to be associated with him again – Binkie's standing in the profession was second to none.

We lunched and both Herbert and I were more than interested in the proposal he put forward. In New York a revival of *No, No, Nanette* had given Ruby Keeler a very great success. Ruby was one of the outstanding Hollywood stars of the 1930s and 1940s with her phenomenal tap dancing. Now, coming back to theatre she had taken New York by storm. How would I feel about playing the part in London? They had planned to put it on at the Theatre Royal, Drury Lane, where I'd not worked since dancing in the chorus of *Desert Song*. It sounded a most exciting venture. But, above all, it was to be presented by Binkie in association with the American producers.

We agreed it would be the perfect follow-up to *Charlie Girl*. We did not get to the contract stage since the show was not planned to go into rehearsal for some months. This meant I could take a good long rest before tackling any preliminary work. But I was still feeling fatigued – not picking up as quickly as I'd expected.

My doctor thought I should have an examination by a a specialist. An appointment was made but, as I was anxious that Herbert should not be worried I told him I was seeing my dentist. The verdict was disturbing. When I saw him again, X-rays and tests were positive and cancer was diagnosed. An immediate operation was necessary.

I suppose I have always been so fit that I've taken good health for granted. It had seemed to me that, given the good constitution I so obviously had, it was up to me to take care of it. Throughout so many years in theatre, films, personal appearance tours, the only time I'd had to take time off for illness was when I contracted a deep-seated attack of bronchitis during *Charlie Girl*. Naturally, with such a tremendously long run, I'd had a yearly holiday break, when Sheila Mathews played for me, and with the absence caused by the bronchitis, my old friend Evelyn Laye had kindly taken over for a few weeks. But, apart from this, I'd just kept going.

Well, now I'd have to break the news to Herbert. I wandered round the garden with Tuppence trying to choose my moment. When I did tell him, he was quite stunned. The date was set for me to go into hospital but we agreed there should be no publicity: I didn't want my relatives and friends to worry about me. This was something I had never contemplated might happen to me.

An eminent surgeon operated, followed by several weeks of intensive treatments. Then, the X-rays were satisfactory. A spell by the sea, some swimming with a short rest each day and I'd be fighting fit. I was – so much so, that I was passed for insurance without a 'loaded' policy.

You will wonder why I reveal this now? My specialist friend feels it may encourage so many not to put off seeking advice too late. 'Take it in time,' he says, so that surgeons can carry out their skilful work and many lives can be saved or the disease possibly prevented from spreading. Many women fear disfigurement. They may even be spared this as I have been.

When I began work on *Nanette* the whole thing was behind me – completely shut out of my mind.

No, No, Nanette ran for eight months. But it seemed fated. Binkie Beaumont died. Herbert and I had lunched with him together with Mrs Cyma Rubin who had presented the show in New York. Rehearsals were well under way and Binkie in fine form. Next morning on the radio we heard the unbelievable news.

As is customary in the theatre, everything carried on as usual. My main work was concentrating on the big tap routine – *I Want to be Happy*. I'd not tap-danced since the 1930s. The choreographer and his assistant were wonderful, so patient and encouraging, as were the boys and girls backing me in the dance sequence. We opened to enthusiastic preview audiences.

Tuppence trod the boards of Drury Lane Theatre. But on the day before the first night of *No, No, Nanette* she disappeared. We had been rehearsing all day and a preview at night. So, I was not told until I got home. Joyce and Herbert had searched the entire neighbourhood, as did I the next morning. Notes were tacked on trees. Sadly I had to leave for the theatre and the opening performance.

At the first interval a call came through to my dressing-room. The small daughter of an actress living nearby had seen the 'Tuppence Missing' notices. They had found her in their garden the previous night and taken her in. Mrs Martin, who helps take care of us at home, was with Joyce 'taking care' of our guests in the theatre. They dropped everything as soon as the curtain went up on the second act, grabbed a taxi and when I came off at the end of the show Tuppence was safely curled up in her usual spot.

In the audience on that first night sitting in the box with Herbert, were two people to whom I feel tremendously indebted – Odette, who has been such an inspiration, and the brilliant surgeon who had operated on me.

Friends were kind. Just what was needed, they felt – a very fine cast, a classic musical comedy score, a happy show. But, as I've said, it seemed fated. The American production team were back in the States, and without the guiding genius of Binkie Beaumont, there was a strangely bewildering vacuum.

For me, there was a great sadness when again, Tuppence was missing – once more, the 'theatre' found her. Another theatrical family who, by happy coincidence, shared our vet, had taken her to him. We had known for some time that she was far from well and sadly he confirmed what we already knew deep down. She was frail and fifteen years old, or thereabouts. In my arms I carried her once more round the garden she so loved. That afternoon, she died. She was buried in a small grave where rosemary is growing in profusion. But it's not necessary to call on the rosemary. Even without it Tuppence will never be forgotten. A small cat, with a vivid, brave, and unforgettable personality.

And then after several months, I tripped up some steps, falling on my knee. I didn't even notice it but there was a step in the routine which was aggravating the slight injury and I was advised I must rest the leg. Footballers know the frustration of a pulled hamstring tendon.

The reaction of audiences to the final scene in *Nanette* was extraordinary. On stage playing ukuleles, the full Company sang *I Want to be Happy* and *Tea for Two*. Invariably, the audience clapped hands to the rhythm and joined in the numbers spontaneously. It was always a happy 'curtain'.

There was another very happy occasion. Herbert, not allowed to climb mountains since his thrombosis at the time of *Charlie Girl*, has compromised by moving them!

Tell Herbert something is impossible, his answer is 'I know – let's have a bash.' He often pulls off the seemingly impossible. Having had such successful Gala performances of *Sixty Glorious Years* at Melbourne and Auckland, he decided to have one in London. He wanted the Odeon, Leicester Square, where in 1938 the Queen Mother, Queen Mary had attended the world première. He hoped Queen Elizabeth the Queen Mother would attend this second Gala performance. To our delight, the Queen Mother graciously consented.

Since Royalty does not patronise the same film twice, I had thought it a hopeless request to make. Sir John Davis, head of the Rank Organisation, not only made the theatre available – the same electric sign appeared outside the Odeon as had been there thirty-five years before. The experienced executives who handle all these Royal occasions were made available and Sir John ensured the financial success of the evening for the two causes which were to benefit – the Imperial Cancer Research and the King Edward VII Hospital.

As I was playing at Drury Lane and our curtain was not down until 10.15 p.m., it seemed I wouldn't be able to meet the Queen Mother as the film would be over by 10.00 p.m Herbert reported this to the Queen Mother's Private Secretary, telling him how terribly disappointed I was. Word came back, almost immediately, that the Queen Mother would be happy for the film to start later so that I could be presented at the end. A lovely gesture.

Herbert made all the arrangements – 'Don't attempt to take off your stage make-up,' he said, 'just get out of the costume, into your dress and get here. I've asked Gillie's husband to be waiting for you at the stage door and he'll drive you and Gillie to the side entrance of the Odeon. You will be met there and taken to the wings! When the final curtain comes down on the film the tabs will close and open again immediately. You will only have seconds to get centre stage, while the tabs are down. A spotlight will hit you as the tabs open again. You curtsey to the Queen Mother and say your piece.'

I should explain that the last scene of *Sixty Glorious Years* is the death of old Queen Victoria in her eighty-second year – the make-up of Guy Pearce, the greatest of all make-up men, was extraordinary. I looked every one of eighty-two years and everyone finds the scene extremely moving.

Within seconds I was standing centre stage in a white sequined dress.

The transformation from the old dying Queen was such that a gasp passed through the audience – they applauded and cheered, many standing.

I waited for the noise to subside but the ovation went on for minutes. and when I tried to say my few words of thanks I could not speak.

However, I somehow managed my piece.

After many curtain calls, the manager came and literally pulled me off the stage to take me to the foyer where the Queen Mother was waiting.

Herbert was with her and she opened her arms to me as she greeted me.

'Thank you for a wonderful evening,' she said. 'A beautiful film – I hope young people will see it!'

She gripped my hand and, as you can see from the picture of our meeting, how emotional it must have been for the Queen Mother, since the late King George VI, by his interest and providing the facilities, made the production possible.

'I trust, Ma'am,' I said to the Queen Mother, 'you will forgive my stage make-up but I had no time.'

'I wish I had some on,' the Queen Mother broke in, 'it would have hidden some of this,' and she pointed to her eyes which were still moist.

That night of November 22nd 1973 will, I know, never fade from my memory.

I have so often been told:

'What a wonderful life you have had. You must write a book about it.'

Well, I have! I hope you have found it interesting. It has been a great experience writing it – giving me an opportunity of reliving the days that have gone – so many wonderful days with some dark patches, of course.

But no regrets.

I want to finish, as I started – hearing the voice of dear Jack Buchanan singing:

> There's always tomorrow to bring us a smile
> Maybe we should borrow that thought for a while.
> Tomorrow we'll borrow a thought from a song.
> To capture the rapture of days that are gone.

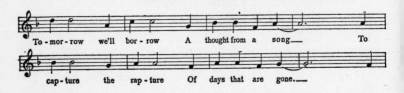

Appendix A

Films

Should a Doctor Tell?
The Chinese Bungalow
Goodnight Vienna
The Flag Lieutenant
The Little Damozel
Bitter Sweet
The Queen's Affair
Nell Gwyn
Peg of Old Drury Lane
Limelight
The Three Maxims
London Melody
Victoria the Great
Sixty Glorious Years
Nurse Edith Cavell
Irene
No, No, Nanette
Sunny
Forever and a Day
They Flew Alone
The Yellow Canary
I Live in Grosvenor Square
Piccadilly Incident
The Courtneys of Curzon Street
Spring in Park Lane

Elizabeth of Ladymead
Maytime in Mayfair
Odette
The Lady with the Lamp
Derby Day
Lilacs in the Spring (*The Glorious Days*)
King's Rhapsody
My Teenage Daughter
No Time for Tears
The Man who Wouldn't Talk
The Lady is a Square

FILMS PRODUCED BY ANNA NEAGLE
These Dangerous Years
Wonderful Things
The Heart of a Man

Appendix B

Stage Appearances

1917	*Wonder Tales (children's play)*
1925	*Bubbly (revival)*
1925	*Charlot's Revue*
1926	*Tricks*
1926	*Rose-Marie*
1926	*The Desert Song*
1926–29	*C. B. Cochran's Trocadero Cabarets*
1927–30	*One Damn Thing After Another*
	This Year of Grace
	Wake Up and Dream (London and New York)
1930–32	*Stand Up and Sing*
1934	*As You Like It, Twelfth Night (Regent's Park)*
1937–38	*Peter Pan*
1942	*Celebrity Parade (in Canada) R.C.A.F.*
1943	*ENSA tour, England.*
1944–45	*Emma*
1945	*French Without Tears (ENSA continental tour)*
1952–53	*The Glorious Days*
1959–60	*The More the Merrier*
1961	*Nothing is for Free (Tour)*
1963–65	*Person Unknown*
1965–71	*Charlie Girl (London)*
1971–72	*Charlie Girl (Melbourne, Auckland)*
1973–74	*No, No, Nanette*

Appendix C

Awards

Josh Billings – Kinematograph: Anna Neagle
awarded the greatest individual acting performance
of the year in *Odette*

1966   VARIETY CLUB 'SPECIAL AWARD' TO ANNA NEAGLE

.

Index